Deanna McKellip

Deanna McKellip

NAMPA
IDAHO
1885 - 1985

A Journey of Discovery

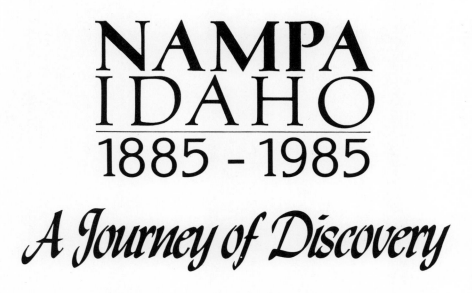

NAMPA
IDAHO
1885 - 1985
A Journey of Discovery

Lynda Campbell Clark

Picture Research by Gerda Ruppert

Sponsored by:
Nampa Centennial Committee
Pacific Press Publishers
Nampa, Idaho

Frontispiece photo by Jim Thomas

Book Design and Layout: Kevin Nelson

Photos provided by the Canyon County Historical
Society (CCHS) and the Idaho State Historical
Society (ISHS) unless otherwise indicated.

Library of Congress Cataloging-in-Publication Data

```
Clark, Lynda Campbell.
   Nampa, Idaho, 1885-1985.

   Includes index.
   1. Nampa (Idaho)--History.  2. Nampa (Idaho)--
Description.  I. Nampa Centennial Committee.  II. Title.
F754.N3C55  1985          979.6'23          85-29698
ISBN 0-8163-0640-0
```

Published in 1985

Printed in the United States of America

First Edition

Contents

I
Nampa's Birth
1885 - 1900

When the government surveyed Township 3 North, Range 2 West of the Boise Meridian district and filed a plat on April 20, 1883, in the United States land office at Boise City, it laid the groundwork which made the establishment of a town possible in the area. In September of 1883, workers put down the rails of the Oregon Short Line, pausing long enough at a desolate spot to erect a water tank, build a section house and put up a small white sign which proclaimed the name, Nampa.

At about the same time, Alexander Duffes sold his merchandising and grain business in Burlington, Canada. He traveled with his family in the Pacific Northwest for a couple of years before he left his family in a residence over a music store in Portland, Oregon. Duffes then explored up and down the coast, searching out a permanent location where he could settle his family and invest his capital.

While in Portland, the Duffes family became acquainted with James A. McGee of Caldwell, Idaho, whose brother-in-law owned the store over which the Duffes' lived. McGee introduced Duffes to Idaho.

James McGee moved West from Pennsylvania in the early 1880's, settling in Caldwell. By 1885, his relations with the developers of the town of Caldwell had become strained. Being a speculator and promoter, he encouraged Duffes to found a new town in order to provide himself with a new place in which to continue his endeavors.

McGee had two things in mind. He planned the building of a canal company to bring irrigation water to the area and he envisioned the rerouting of the branch line connecting Boise to the Oregon Short Line. Caldwell had already obtained the right-of-way and had graded seven miles of land along the Boise River for the line when Nampa came into existence.

McGee convinced Duffes that Nampa offered a land of promise. On November 11, 1885, Alexander Duffes, speculating on

Alexander Duffes, the founder of Nampa, took out a homestead in November of 1885 on the land where Nampa is now located. (Courtesy, Jerry Cornilles)

Facing page: In the Nampa area prior to 1885, an unknown homesteader pauses from clearing sagebrush near what is now Lake Lowell. (CCHS)

JAS. A. McGEE, NAMPA, IDAHO.

Duffes was enticed to the area by James McGee, a promoter who had become disgruntled with the neighboring town of Caldwell. (CCHS)

the development of a town, filed under the Homestead Act on the land where Nampa is now located, the west half of Southeast quarter of section 22 and the North half of Northeast quarter of section 27 in Township 3 North and 2 West, and began building a four-room house there.

In 1926, Duffes looked back on the selection of the townsite:

> I came to Caldwell and drove around three or four weeks and picked out a point in the country where I thought would be a good townsite. That was right here at Nampa. I built a four room house in 1885 where the brewery is now, (on Ninth Avenue between First and Second streets north) and that was the first home here except the section house at the corner of Front Street and Thirteenth Avenue.

On July 19, 1886, Duffes "proved up" on his homestead after living on the land for eight months by paying a dollar and twenty-five cents per acre or $200 total. Then Duffes, McGee and James M. Stewart organized "The Nampa Land and Improvement Company," commonly called the "Townsite Company," and filed the plat and Articles of Incorporation for the town on September 8, 1886.

The Caldwell Tribune, referring to Nampa, noted on October 2, 1886:

This early photo shows the residence of James McGee. The flume of the Phyllis Canal is in the background. (Courtesy, Jerry Cornilles)

> "New Jerusalem" has been surveyed and laid out into town lots. Several purchases have been made already, and the projectors seem to think the town is now an assured fact. It hasn't been christened yet, but there is time enough for that by and by.

Left: In l885 Duffes built a four-room house on Ninth Avenue close to First Street North where the brewery was later located. It was later enlarged and remodeled. Maude Duffes and daughter Eva pose here on the porch of the Duffes home. (ISHS)

Below: When the Nampa Chamber of Commerce agreed to furnish a suitable site for the building of a brewery in town, the Duffes home was moved across the street and again remodeled. The original location of the Duffes homestead became the site of Nampa's brewery. (ISHS)

But Caldwell had already lost its first citizen to Nampa. In May of 1886 the Caldwell paper reported that its editor, W. J. Cuddy, was leaving to become a "New Jerusalem" farmer. James McGee was more cautious, however. He waited until September of 1887 to move his family from Caldwell to Nampa.

The development of Nampa was underway. Building began immediately after the filing of the plat in the fall of 1886 and in three months time "ninety-two lots had been sold to twenty-six different firms and individuals, and twenty-four teams and forty men were working on the ditches."

In 1891 the town of Nampa contained several residential and commercial structures, grouped together in the midst of sagebrush. (ISHS)

And so McGee and Duffes made a good bet, or so it seemed, by speculating on the development of a town at Nampa. But, why Nampa? Why this location?

Fenton G. Cottingham, self-styled Nampa historian, answered this question in 1912 when he wrote: "When the Oregon Short Line Railroad was built through Nampa, the foundation of the town was built and when water was turned into the Ridenbaugh and Phyllis ditches the cornerstone was laid." Thus, two major developments brought the town of Nampa into fruition: the railroad and the canals which brought irrigation. With these enterprises, Nampa was "christened."

Advertisements such as these were circulated in the East and the Midwest by the Oregon Short Line Railroad in order to entice settlers to the area. Some of the ads were fraudulent because they promoted the region as an agricultural community while the land surrounding Nampa was still covered with sagebrush. (ISHS)

THE RAILROAD

In 1883 when the railroad constructed the Oregon Short Line through Idaho, the only town between Mountain Home and the mouth of the Burnt River was Boise, the capital of Idaho. But the railroad engineers by-passed Boise for three reasons: the line would have had to be about eight miles longer; the terrain was very rough going into Boise causing additional cost; and the citizens of Boise refused to contribute $10,000 toward the enterprise.

Passengers headed for Boise took the stage line from Kuna, a "hot, dusty, jolting trip" over unimproved trails. A connecting line between the Oregon Short Line and Boise was inevitable.

As early as 1885, promoters made plans to build a connecting line from the Oregon Short Line to Boise. Caldwell obtained the necessary right of ways and began grading, but the case for starting the branch line at Nampa had unquestionable merits: it would be ten miles shorter and require less grading and maintenance than the Caldwell river route. James McGee, anxious to take the line away from Caldwell, "went to Boston and returned with the branch line in his pocket." He also brought back General J.F. Curtis of Boston, a railroad official.

On June 26, 1886, less than a month before Alexander Duffes proved up on his homestead, the Idaho Central Railway Company was incorporated at Cheyenne, Wyoming, with its purpose being to build a branch line from Nampa to Boise and to make Nampa "the transportation center of Southwestern Idaho."

It was significant, of course, that James McGee was president of the Nampa Townsite Company and its general manager. He, along with James Stewart, the vice president and treasurer of the Townsite Company, served as trustees in the Idaho Central Railroad and organized the Phyllis Canal Company. The success of the townsite depended on the development of both of these enterprises.

By December of 1886, the Oregon Short Line railroad clearly

Before the branch line railroad was built between Nampa and Boise, passengers headed for the capital city had to take a stage line from Kuna over unimproved trails. (ISHS)

Nampa's first train depot, used until 1903, was located at Thirteenth and Front streets. (CCHS)

The Idaho Central Railway Company built the branch line between Nampa and Boise. The first train arrived at the Boise Depot on September 1, 1887. (ISHS)

The first freight depot for the railroad was located between Fifteenth and Sixteenth Avenues on Front Street. The coal chute is visible at the left. This picture was taken in June of 1896. (ISHS)

The railroad was constructed by horse team between Nampa and Boise, (ISHS)

Below: For years Nampa was called "Junction City" because of the railroad activity in the town. (ISHS)

The railroad connected Nampa with the rest of the world. Here we see engine number one of the Southern Pacific with an Oregon Short Line train in the background. (ISHS)

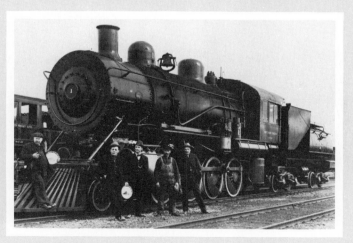

Helen Milliken Payne Barney, a long-time Nampa resident, recalls the excitement of the trains: "The big black locomotives were thrilling, with smoke rolling out of their big smokestacks. At night the sound of the train whistles carried a long distance and it was a very musical sound, though mournful." (ISHS)

supported the new town. The Boise newspaper noted:

> It is reported that the new town is to have the support, encouragement and patronage of the Oregon Short Line railroad, and that it is to be made the end of a division. That ought to give the place a big boost and send the town forward at a rapid rate. Such an event will be cold comfort to the people of Caldwell who have invested large sums of money in buildings under similar promises. The townsite business seems to be the favorite means of speculation on the part of the Oregon Short Line and Union Pacific

Simultaneously, the development of the town and the branch line moved forward. A railroad engineer with his assistant and railroad surveying equipment not only worked for the railroad, but surveyed and helped lay out the new town.

In September of 1887 the train reached Boise. The Idaho Statesman reported that the track layers moved "a little in advance" of the construction train "laying down the ties and rails." Howard E. King, fireman on the first train, reminisced about the experience:

> I recall that the work train to Boise carried both passengers and freight, and that the train crew always found their seats occupied by passengers who would crowd into the engine. I never had a chance to sit in the fireman's seat. Boise was just a hamlet and almost the entire populace swarmed on the hill to see the first train. Many never before had seen steam cars, having crossed the plains before the coming of the railroad and the sight was wonderful to them. We incited as much curosity then as a modern circus parade would today.

McGee fulfilled his ambition to have a branch line between Nampa and Boise, but it was not as easy for him to bring irrigation to the area.

THE COMING OF IRRIGATION

The train alone was not sufficient to support the citizens of Nampa. The land carried promise of producing fruits and vegetables. An optimistic early report on the town from Caldwell noted that the "crops are looking first-class." But, initially "it was impossible to make a living on the land." Generally speaking, the women and children stayed on the homestead while the men went to work elsewhere, many of them associated with the Oregon Short Line.

An early settler reported:

> Water was so scarce that people would plant
> grass seed when they saw clouds in the sky in
> the hopes that there might be sufficient rain to
> cause it to grow. . . . Until trees began to
> grow, there seemed to be no birds, just owls,
> and everything was so dry and desolate.

Drinking water was obtained by drilling wells but even this was not always predictable. Duffes had to drill twice to find water for his first house, going down sixty feet the first time. He moved a short distance away and tried again, this time striking water in nine feet.

Promises of water were abundant. The April 6, 1886 edition of the Caldwell Tribune speculated, "Don't know much about the townsite (Nampa); but can say there will be a fine ditch and water galore." When McGee talked Duffes into founding the town, he contended that water would be available in six months.

By 1891, Nampa was hot and dry and the citizens of the town were desperate. They had heard of successful efforts to produce rainfall in Texas, Arizona and New Mexico. Being tired of the hot and dusty climate, Nampans began to correspond with Frank

Water was scarce when Nampa was established. Sagebrush covered everything. (CCHS)

The Morris ditch, started in 1877, was inherited by William H. Ridenbaugh. He sold the property to a Boise-based organization in 1889 for $60,000. Water reached Nampa in the Ridenbaugh Canal in May of 1892. (ISHS)

Melborn of Australia, a famous rainmaker. He agreed to produce for Nampa and the surrounding area up to a fifty mile radius one-half inch of rain. He charged five hundred dollars.

F. G. Cottingham related the story:

> He came on September 22nd. There was an air of mystery about his looks and movements that immediately challenged attention. School children kept on the other side of the street and spoke in whispers. About 10 o'clock A.M. he took a small tent and went onto the roof of the building at the corner of 11th Avenue and 1st Street, the one where the Leader is now published, set up his tent with a small stove pipe in one end and retired from view.

> The rest of that day was one of suppressed excitement: the conversation was carried on with bated breath; no one went near the building. At sundown that night, far in the west were two small clouds: at 9 P.M. he gave it up, folded his tent and vanished.

Not until 1892 did water reach Nampa through the irrigation canals, but bringing water to desert lands was not as easy as early Nampa developers envisioned. The irrigation canal companies underwent numerous ownership changes and experienced severe financial difficulties.

The Morris ditch, started in 1877, was inherited by W.H. Ridenbaugh. He sold the property to a Boise-based organization in 1889 for $60,000. In about a year it changed owners again, this time being bought out by eastern capitalists. Water reached Nampa in the Ridenbaugh Canal in May of 1892. But shortly after this, the property changed hands two more times. After being owned by New York capitalists, the canal company was bought in 1905 by the Nampa Meridian Irrigation district for $205,000.

James McGee and J.M. Stewart, members of the original Townsite Company, attempted to develop the Phyllis Canal Company, named after McGee's curly-haired daughter, Mary

James M. Stewart and James A. McGee incorporated the Phyllis Canal Company, shown here in the construction stage, in November of 1885. Its purpose was to provide water to the Nampa area for agricultural and mining purposes. (CCHS)

In 1892 water reached Nampa through the Phyllis Canal. Water ran through ditches which were located in the midst of sagebrush. (ISHS)

This pipeline serviced the Phyllis Canal. It was a 500-feet long, four-foot drain and yielded fifty-four cubic feet of pressure. (ISHS)

In 1902 the Pioneer Irrigation Company purchased the Phyllis Canal Company. This picture of the Phyllis Canal was taken around 1905. (ISHS: Donated by Dr. Raymond J. Bungard)

Phyllis, but found the going rough. They obtained financial backing from a banker and his associates in Philadelphia and commenced work on the canal in 1886. After constructing about two miles of the irrigation canal, the company was overcome by financial troubles. The project lay dormant until 1889 when it was taken over by the New York Canal Company. Before the canal could be completed, the company went bankrupt. Local contractors filed a lien and in the foreclosure of the company, became the owners of the canal. In 1892 water reached Nampa through the Phyllis Canal. In 1902 the Pioneer Irrigation Company purchased the enterprise.

More than five years after it was initially thought possible, Nampa had irrigation water. Farming was now possible on the land surrounding the town of Nampa and the cornerstone of the town was laid.

Work on the Phyllis Canal began in 1886, but when the company was overcome by financial difficulties, the project lay dormant until 1889. Workers used horse drawn equipment in building the Nampa irrigation canals. (CCHS)

LIFE IN EARLY NAMPA

An ingenious entrepreneur developed a sagebrush grubber to be pulled behind horses to help remove the unwanted plant. (ISHS)

Life in Nampa and the surrounding countryside was not easy in the 1880s. Those who were homesteading found their land covered with sagebrush. Before farm ground could be laid out or dwellings built, the sagebrush had to be removed. Often railroad ties were pulled behind horses in order to clear the ground. One homesteader remembered that he "attacked" the sagebrush for days on end.

When money was in short supply, sagebrush served as a substitute. Because it was used in stoves in place of wood, there was some demand for sagebrush among the townfolks. Homesteaders would cut, trim and bundle the plant and then either sell it or exchange it for needed supplies.

In town the streets were simply dirt roads which had been made by "hitching ten or twelve horses to a rail and striking out across the brush." After a rainstorm, the mud and pools of water made the streets nearly impassable. When the rain failed to fall, the

The Nampa area was initially covered by sagebrush-desert. (ISHS)

George Karcher, Sr., poses in 1892. (ISHS)

jackrabbits ventured out into the hot and dusty Nampa streets and alleys. Some Nampans took advantage of the fact that Ada County offered a bounty of five cents for a pair of jackrabbit ears.

Western towns in their early stages of development had a reputation for catering to the common vices of life, in particular, drinking, gambling and prostitution. Nampa was no exception.

Saloons were established in the town before churches. In 1887, the "itemizer," as he called himself, for the Boise Statesman, noted that Nampa was "a fine location" although it "had neither church nor preacher." That failed to concern him. "We can get along for awhile without either if we only have a barber, a drug store, a blacksmith shop, and a doctor, although there is no sickness yet." However, the town did have two saloons --- the "itemizer" was the proprietor of one of them --- and a third saloon was built later that same year.

Ironically, in the beginning, the surrounding towns of Boise

George Karcher and his wife Elizabeth homesteaded on the present site of Karcher Mall. Their children James and Louis are shown in front of the house. The milk house is on the left. (ISHS)

and Caldwell referred to Nampa as the "New Jerusalem" because Alexander Duffes hoped to keep saloons out of the town. Being a Presbyterian and a teetotaler, Duffes refused to sell town lots to people who planned to build saloons on them. Those who failed to share Duffes' convictions circumvented his desires by buying lots which were initially purchased for other purposes. Duffes had no control over these third party transactions.

By 1892 when the first Chamber of Commerce was organized, drinking of alcoholic beverages was an established fact of social life in the town. Cottingham reports:

> We published the fact that we were ready to
> build railroads, irrigation canals, fruit
> evaporators, ice plants, creameries,
> everything, even to mint juleps. Well, the
> boys built more of the last named article than
> the others . . .

In 1905, the Chamber endorsed the building of a brewery in Nampa by agreeing to furnish a suitable site. Ironically, the location was the site of Duffes first dwelling, which was moved across the street.

Drinking was not the only vice in town during the early days of Nampa. Nampa had plenty of gambling houses and at least one house of prostitution which was established sometime before 1891. During this year some concerned citizens presented a petition for "social betterment" to the village trustees, asking that "houses of questionable character" be suppressed. The council rejected their request, however, ordering the petition "to be laid under the table."

In October of 1905 the chief of police was called to the local "bawdy house" because the proprietor feared that "a girl called May" had been poisoned. After calling in physicians who found "no trace of poison," the authorities concluded that her illness was "doubtless being caused from a protracted spree or the administration of dope." She would recover, they said.

In December of 1906 Nampa's house of prostitution was again

in the news. This time tragedy struck when six young men from Boise came to Nampa on the midnight train seeking a good time. They went directly to the "bawdy house" on H street where they were well acquainted and "a hilarious time ensued." All was well until Grace Herion, a resident of the house, pulled out "an old Bull Dog revolver" which accidentally discharged, striking one of the Boise visitors in the abdomen and seriously wounding him. The Leader-Herald reported:

> Daily fell to the floor and the girl realizing what she had done, rushed frantically into her room exclaiming: "My God, I have shot Tom and I will kill myself." Before the other inmates could reach her she had placed the muzzle to her left temple and pulled the trigger, killing herself instantly.

Local authorities ruled the man's shooting purely accidental and reports from Boise where Tom Daily was taken indicated that he would probably recover.

Perhaps it was the reputation of Nampa's house of prostitution that motivated the editor of the Owyhee Avalanche to call Nampa a "very, very wicked town." Although initial attempts to close down prostitution in Nampa failed, by 1906 city officials were ready to try actively to regulate saloons, gambling and prostitution.

In November of that year a cigar store on Front Street was closed by Mayor R.W. Purdum because gambling had become a frequent activity there. "This place has been in ill repute for some time," the local newspaper commented. "Places where young boys, especially, are allowed to go and gamble are dens of iniquity which no self respecting community will tolerate in this day and age," they added.

A few months later the city council passed an ordinance prohibiting boys under the age of sixteen from frequenting billiard halls and fining proprietors of such establishments if young boys

The Pullman Bar was located in the 100 block of Twelfth Avenue South. This picture was taken around 1895. (CCHS)

The interior of the Pullman Bar is shown in 1890. Owner Frank Wenzel is behind the bar. (CCHS)

Cigar stores were a common place of business and entertainment. Some of the stores had pool tables. (CCHS)

were found on their premises. Again, the newspaper endorsed the action, contending, "Billiard halls are just as unfit, if not more so than saloons since it is in such places that the most of evil habits are formed [sic]."

Less than a year later the town turned its attention to the saloons in Nampa. Because there were complaints that one or two saloons had been selling liquor to minors, the city council passed an ordinance requiring the removal of all screens and other obstructions from the doors and windows of establishments selling alcoholic beverages so that the policemen could better view the interior of such places of business without entering them. This ordinance also required a midnight closing hour for the saloons, some of which had been staying open all night.

When Edward H. Dewey became mayor in 1909, records show that prostitution was still practiced in Nampa. However, Dewey promised to keep it under control. He announced:

> In the red light district there will be no compromise with crime. No fee or fine will be exacted of the unfortunate inhabitants of that section, nor will they be driven out of their usual haunts to be scattered through the respectable parts of the city. They will be kept segregated so far as possible and not allowed to flaunt themselves upon the streets. These matters the police will be expected to look after carefully.

Although Nampa tolerated drinking, gambling and prostitution in its early days, it also saw the establishment of churches early in its history. Nampa's first church building was constructed in 1889, almost three years after the incorporation of the town. The Townsite Company donated the lot and a public subscription raised money for the construction. George Buzzell, a lay reader in the Episcopal Church, provided the impetus for the completion of this building, but until it was dedicated two years later, it was used by all denominations for services.

Congregations began developing before their buildings were erected, however. In the case of the Brethren, church members were actively solicited to help settle the town. In the fall of 1897, D.E. Burley, an early agent for the Oregon Short Line, made contact with Samuel Bock, a Brethren layman in Dayton, Ohio, and encouraged him to visit several prospective farming areas along the railroad. Bock, in turn, became an emigration agent employed by the Oregon Short Line from 1898 to 1911 and was responsible for the migration of hundreds of Brethren to the Snake River Valley.

In November of 1899, J. H. Graybill, a Brethren minister, migrated from Roanoke, Virginia and along with E. J. Fogle, organized the Nampa Brethren congregation with an initial membership of twelve. Graybill also became an agent for the Oregon Short Line, supplementing his income in this manner. By 1912, the Brethren congregation numbered ninety.

At the turn of the century, four churches had buildings --- the Presbyterians, Episcopalians, Baptists and Catholics --- and the Methodists, Brethren, and Mennonites had organized societies. By 1906 a church census gave the following church affiliations: Catholic, 28; Christian, 21; Baptist, 30; Episcopalian, 37; German Baptist, 43; Presbyterian, 61; and Methodist, 97.

The Episcopal Church was the first church building constructed in Nampa. It was later remodeled and moved. (ISHS)

The Huntleys owned the first grocery stores in Nampa, located at 1111 First Street South. This 1898 photo shows Mr. Sites, Frank Huntley, Mr. Austin, L. G. Huntley, Herman Huntley and Max Hampton in front of the store. (CCHS)

By 1910, Nampa's first grocery store had been moved to Front Street. Ed Huntley, Claude Collier, a boy named Tuffy, Frank Page and Ed Page stand in front of the store. (CCHS)

Below: Located on the corner of Front Street and Eleventh Avenue South, this building was constructed in 1887 by Dr. F.S. Kohler who used it as a drug store and office. Shown are Mrs. Emma Kesl; Frank Estabrook, Sr.; Frank Burns, a clerk in the store; Sam Bassam, father of Mrs. Kesl; S. S. Taylor, who looks the part of the city constable but supposedly joined the Soapy Smith Gang; Dr. F. S. Kohler; O. F. Persons, who built Lake Ethel; and Creed Click, Jr. (Courtesy, Jerry Cornilles)

WOMEN IN EARLY NAMPA

Early in Nampa's history, women played an important role in the development of the town, even to the point of homesteading land. Mrs. J.S. Hickey, the first woman to hold down land under the Homestead Act, took up residence in Nampa December 6, 1886.

Equal suffrage became effective early in Idaho's history. When Idaho became a state in 1890, its constitution provided women the right to vote. Idaho was one of the first states to allow women this right.

Nampa women took this duty seriously. In 1896 the women of Nampa ran their own candidate for the school board. Mrs. Simpson had no opposition but "it was whispered around that the men were going to elect some one else." Being new voters who "were young and easily scared," the women of the town reacted with vigor. "Teams were hurried into the field and many women interviewed voters." The result: Mrs. Simpson was elected with seventy-nine votes while two men received one vote each.

In January of 1900 the women of the community founded an organization through which they could channel their efforts toward community betterment, the Woman's Century Club. Its primary purpose was the formation of a library, and at this venture they were eventually successful.

The first library in Nampa consisted of a traveling collection of books which the ladies of the Century Club obtained from the Idaho State Traveling Library. This collection was distributed first through the Nampa Development Company, then through the Cottingham Lumber Yard and finally was available at the Idaho Leader newspaper office.

In June of 1904 when Mrs. Frank Estabrook became chairman of the library committee of the Century Club, her committee requested that the city council levy a tax of one mill on each dollar of assessed valuation of city property in order to establish and

The early Nampa residence of Jacob and Polly Miller was located at 1024 Fourteenth Avenue South. Their children Frank, Ed and Elva pose in the picture. (ISHS)

The Woman's Century Club promoted community projects, including the establishment of a library. Here some of the members pose in historic costumes. (CCHS)

maintain a library. The city pared the tax down to a half mill before granting the request.

In the interim, until the tax money became available, the Century Club opened the library in two rooms of the Hickey Building and paid for its maintenance. The Club charged an annual card fee of one dollar for those wishing to check out books. In 1907 when city support became sufficient, Ennis McGee replaced the volunteers who had been running the library and as a paid librarian earned twenty-five dollars per month. The rent for the two rooms which contained the library amounted to twenty dollars per month. This was the beginning of a city-financed library.

The Century Club Library Committee succeeded in obtaining a commitment from Andrew Carnegie for $10,000 for a public library building provided that the city furnish a lot and guarantee $1000 a year for library maintenance. The city agreed to these terms and appointed a committee to oversee the project.

The appointment of the second committee put the Century Club up in arms. After they protested in vain to the city council, the club sought the attorney general's opinion in the matter. James H. Hawley wrote the opinion and concurred with the Century Club that the committee appointed by the city council was illegal. The control of the new library project was back in the hands of the Century Club but they agreed to cooperate with the city council.

The library moved into the new building in February of 1908 and an open house in the Nampa Carnegie Library occurred March 7, 1908. By June of 1908 the library proudly announced that it had 1312 books in its collection and had served 1369 patrons during the past month.

The Nampa Carnegie Library opened in February of 1908. That year it proudly announced a book collection of 1312 volumes. (CCHS)

The Century Club continued to be an active force in the Nampa community. In 1912, F.G. Cottingham proclaimed that the women of the Century Club "have accomplished more than any other organization that Nampa has ever had; the municipality not excepted."

Evidently, single women were in short supply in Nampa's first year, for the first wedding in Nampa involved a "mail-order" bride. In September of 1887 John Rinker, who lived on a ranch on Upper Reynolds Creek in Owyhee County, married Ann Snively of

Fostoria, Ohio. They had been corresponding after being introduced through a matrimonial agency. Meeting in Nampa for the first time, they spent an hour "in taking a mental inventory of each other" and then "concluded to go ahead with the services." Cottingham described the ceremony:

> All the available population were hastily summoned as witnesses to the hotel parlor; George Bowman, the justice of the peace, was sent for, who performed the ceremony. The groom was so well pleased with his acquisition that he gave the justice $15.00 for the job, which we contend was too much money for a knot that slipped. The happy couple took a wedding trip to Boise, assisted by rice, old shoes, jokes and the best wishes of the crowd.

THE CHINESE IN EARLY NAMPA

The Chinese were an intricate part of the population of Nampa in the town's early days. Imported from China to work on the transcontinental railroad, they moved to the mining camps, in particular in Nevada and Oregon, when work on the railroad was finished. They came to Idaho, as did others, to prospect gold. From the Idaho gold mines they fanned out to settle in the state's developing communities.

They were not always welcome, however. Nampa's neighboring town of Caldwell conducted an active anti-Chinese crusade in 1886, only three years after the town's founding. In October of 1887, a year after Nampa was incorporated, the Statesman reported with some sense of satisfaction that "Nampa was not yet belessee with heathen Chinne."

But their absence in the town was not to remain the case. By

At one time the Chinese community in Nampa numbered approximately one hundred people, all of them male. This photo of the Chinese in a wagon was taken in the Nampa area. (ISHS)

Many of the Chinese in Nampa worked as gardeners and sold their produce door-to-door from baskets which hung at each end of a pole that they carried on their shoulders, similar to this Chinese who is peddling vegetables in another Idaho community. (ISHS)

1892 six Chinese lived in Nampa, according to early records. This number grew until the Chinese community numbered approximately one hundred, all of the male sex, at the peak of its population.

Not unlike other places, Nampa also engaged in expressions of racial prejudice against the Chinese. The first reported incident occurred in 1892 when half a dozen young men decided to drive the Chinese and Japanese from the town. Approximately four hundred Japanese had been brought into the town to do special railroad construction work. Because the Chinese community was smaller, the rebel-rousers began with them.

Nampa's early historian, F.G. Cottingham, remembered:

> They broke in a door to a laundry on 13th avenue. A Chinaman was sleeping in the back part and when the crash came he thought it

was one of the demons from the mountains after him. He grabbed his clothes, jumped through a window and started up the street yelling, the sash to the window not being very secure, in the frame went with him [sic].

After this "victory," the "noble band" approached another laundry on the north side of town. Their experience here was not so gratifying.

When the door was busted in a flat iron in the hand of one of the inmates found the head of one of the assailants who immediately retired to a nearby ditch to remove the gore. He had no sooner begun than a bullet dug up the earth all too close. He flew as well as the balance of the band of hope.

Mostly, the Chinese had to endure thoughtless provocations upon themselves and their property by those who failed to respect their race. Boys supposedly teased the Chinese laundrymen by "throwing dirt or tomatoes at the clothes on the lines on top of the laundries" or by trying to cut the lines with pliers.

In January of 1908 one such nuisance incident was labelled "A Cowardly Piece of Business" by the local newspaper. Someone deliberately, without provocation, threw a rock through a window of a Chinese store on Wall Street and struck an old Chinese who was sitting inside with several others. The old man had one tooth knocked out. The paper reported that this sort of thing had become quite common, but condemned it severely. Although the perpetrators escaped punishment in this incident, "the offenders will be caught some time and when they are they should receive the limit of the law," the newspaper story said.

Although the Chinese came to Idaho to engage in mining careers, when they settled in Idaho's towns they generally found work in the service occupations. In Nampa, the Chinese engaged in one of four different occupations. They were either "house boys," hired for domestic help by some of Nampa's families; gardeners; laundrymen; or restaurant owners. The gardeners maintained their gardens along Indian Creek, watering their plants by hand and marketing their produce door-to-door from baskets which hung at each end of a pole that they carried on their shoulders. Nampans referred to the Chinese laundries as "wash houses" and the Chinese restaurants as "noodle joints."

The Chinese added some cultural diversity to Nampa in its early days. Most of the men still wore queues and "while they dressed in American style on the streets, they preferred and usually wore Oriental costumes indoors."

Until 1901, Sam Sing's laundry on F Street, later Twelfth Avenue and First Street North, was the center of the Chinese community in town. The living quarters behind the laundry contained little side rooms which held bunks used for sleeping and, reportedly, the smoking of opium pipes. Basement rooms with earth walls also contained bunks.

In January of 1901 fire wiped out the building housing Sam Sing's laundry. Two Chinese lost their lives and Sam, the

Most of the Chinese still wore queues and although they dressed in Western clothing when they went out, they usually wore their traditional Oriental dress indoors. (ISHS)

proprietor, was badly burned. Four others escaped without injury. The cause of the fire was unknown, but it was believed that the seven Chinese who occupied the building "were carousing and drinking during the night, or had their senses dulled by opium." A considerable sum of money was lost in the fire. One Chinese had $5000 buried under the building. Observers to the fire found $100 in gold and, supposedly, Nampa police officers found more.

After the fire at Sam's laundry, Chinese headquarters moved to Wall Street. At one time, four Chinese laundries were located in this block. The area was notorious, according to Nampa's early historian, for opium smoking and gambling. Cottingham recalls:

> The alley through Block 7 was called Wall Alley. There were four Chinese wash houses in this block. Wong Duck's place was at the rear of Frank Randall's building. This was a notorious opium joint and the meeting place of Fan Tan players. Some of the biggest games of Southern Idaho were played here. China boys from the Owyhee country, from Boise, Idaho City and Placerville, met here and the sky was the limit as to bets. And they used to say the Alley was the sleeping place for those who went broke.

Fred G. Mock, a well known early Nampa citizen, claimed to have toured the Chinese tunnels and dens which ran under a portion of Nampa's business district. Here Mock poses in an 1897 Masonic Grand Lodge photo. (ISHS)

Many Nampans had heard rumors about tunnels and opium dens under the Chinese establishments, but Fred Mock, an early Nampa citizen, claimed to have toured the tunnels with Lee Sing as his guide. He said he entered the tunnels which were about two feet wide and maybe three feet high through the Commercial Hotel basement. When they reached a "den," the area broadened to about fifteen feet wide in the center and maybe eighteen feet long. The roof was about six or seven feet high and supported by planks which rested on posts. "Bunks had been dug along the sides where smokers curled up," according to Mock.

Outside of the earthen basement tunnels, a large pipe ran up one side of a store, reaching up twenty feet from the ground. No one thought much about this, but Mock speculated that the pipe ventilated the den.

Officers knew of an extensive "dope ring" that spread out to Silver City and Jordan Valley on the South and reached as far as Boise, Idaho City, Placerville and Centerville to the North. "A peddler was arrested now and then but the ring leaders were never caught," said Mock.

In 1909 when the block which contained Wall Street was destroyed by fire, the tunnels and den under the block probably collapsed. Mock claims to have been an eye witness to a scene in which four or five young Chinese men failed to escape from the hot ashes and burning cinders which surrounded the exits of the underground caverns. After the fire, "there was very little traffic in dope for a long time," according to Mock.

After the fire of 1909, the Chinese population in Nampa diminished rapidly. In addition to the fire, perhaps a "tong war" which broke out among the Chinese in Boise in January of 1910 also encouraged them to leave the area. The local newspaper reported that Nampa's Chinese population numbered about forty at this time and since practically all of them belonged to some society or tong, they were "panic stricken" when they learned of the "war" in Boise. "Their first impulse was to flee," said the paper, but the Nampa chief of police assured them that "if they stayed they would be guaranteed protection." All incoming trains were to be watched and any new Chinese entering the town were to be placed under arrest "if they cannot give a good account of themselves."

Nevertheless, by 1917 the Chinese community in Nampa numbered only approximately twenty people and by 1919 only one laundry and one restaurant run by the Chinese remained.

Mock said he entered the Chinese tunnels through the basement of the Commercial hotel. The hotel burned in the 1909 fire which also probably caused the collapse of the Chinese underground tunnels. (ISHS)

II Business Development: 1890 - 1910

At the beginning of the decade in 1890, Nampa experienced continued business development. That year saw the addition of three areas to the original townsite, the building of the Inter-state Hotel on the corner of Thirteenth Avenue and Second Street, the completion of Nampa's first brick building on the corner of Front and Thirteenth Avenue South, and the opening in December of the town's first financial institution, the First Bank of Nampa.

However, by the end of the year Nampa received a "stunning blow." Boasting of a populace of at least 1200, Nampa citizens were taken back when the census report set the town's population at only 347. "Our indignation knew no bounds," said F. G. Cottingham. Financially, the town also soon experienced disappointment. The nationwide panic of 1893 precipitated serious trouble for the Townsite Company.

In May of 1894 Alexander Duffes borrowed $4000 from a man named Rufus Ramsey who was then treasurer of the state of Illinois. The loan was secured by a mortgage on the unsold lots of the Townsite Company. But Ramsey had his own financial troubles. When he defaulted on his personal loans, "the note given by Duffes became a part of the assets to be liquidated to pay creditors." Neither the Duffes family nor the Townsite Company had the ready cash to pay off the note.

By 1896 Ramsey's creditors secured a judgment on the Duffes note amounting to $6644. Colonel W. H. Dewey, a miner and speculator from Silver City, bid $6000 for the note and bailed out the Nampa Townsite Company. A second judgment against the Townsite Company was set aside by the court after an appearance by William E. Borah, Dewey's lawyer. In the deal, Dewey gained possession of over 2000 lots in the town of Nampa.

COLONEL WILLIAM H. DEWEY

Who was this man that became Nampa'a benefactor and why

Facing page: The majestic Dewey Palace distinguished the town of Nampa from 1903 until it was razed in 1963. (ISHS)

Colonel William H. Dewey, a miner and speculator from Silver City, became Nampa's benefactor in 1896 when he paid $6000 for the unsold lots of the Nampa Townsite Company, rescuing the town from financial woes. (ISHS)

was he interested in Nampa? William H. Dewey was born August 1, 1823, in Adams, Massachusetts. When he was three years old, his family moved to a farm in New York state, fifty-two miles from Buffalo.

Dewey's father died in an election day fight which he was trying to stop. He bled to death after being accidentally struck in the wrist with a knife. Dewey's mother was reputed to be "almost unbearably cranky of a morning until she had eaten her breakfast." One morning when she slapped William and ordered him outside to milk the cows, he ran away. Without shoes, underclothing or an overcoat, he walked the fifty-two miles to Buffalo, New York, in three or four days. He was only eleven years old at the time.

In Buffalo, William got a job which paid two dollars a week plus room and board driving a mule on the Erie Canal. His son, Con, later reported that by the time he was fifteen, he had two barges of his own. He moved to Tonawanda, New York, where he built a penny arcade, the first in the United States, and owned a saw mill, a shingle mill and a livery stable.

There is some speculation that Dewey also made money by smuggling horses from Canada. The horses cost Dewey a dollar a piece but were resold for a profit of eight to thirteen dollars a head. Dewey and his partner Tom Gillesay swam horses at night to an island Dewey had bought in the Niagara River where they fed them and resold them in a few days.

By the time he was twenty, Dewey had amassed a $20,000 fortune, but although he made large sums of money, he also spent it "with a lavish hand." Thus, when he was nearly forty, Dewey, searching for more lucrative territory, headed to San Francisco. It took him nearly fourteen months to make the boat trip because he contracted malaria and was put off the ship in Nicaragua.

Once in San Francisco, he began a contracting business with Michael Jordan, but soon the men were drawn by the stories of rich gold strikes in Virginia City, Nevada. There Dewey and Jordan struck out. Their $160,000 capital dwindled to $3100 after they played the stock market and bought worthless mining claims.

Again they heard the cries of easy wealth, this time in the mining areas of Idaho. Jordan left Virginia City ahead of Dewey because Dewey was suffering another bout with malaria. Then in 1863, Jordan sent word to Dewey that Idaho mines contained great potential for money-making.

Dewey "on foot and weighing 135 pounds at five feet seven and a half, started on the lonesome 400-mile trek over the wastelands on August 27, with twenty-seven dollars in his pocket." He arrived in the mountains of Owyhee County November 24, 1863, with "no shoes on his feet." Within seven years, Dewey struck it rich, while his partner, Michael Jordan, was killed by Indians. By 1870, Dewey owned half of the successful South Mountain camp.

Dewey, the "promoter, builder and organizer" was flamboyant and venturesome, "sometimes to the point of recklessness." In 1884 Dewey's recklessness caught up with him. The day after a bar room argument with Henry Koenig, the bartender, Dewey followed Koenig from the saloon down the hill to the brewery, reportedly at Koenig's request. There a shoot-out occurred. Dewey claimed he was taken off-guard and responded in self-defense, but when the

In search of adventure and wealth, W. H. Dewey travelled by foot to Silver City from Virginia City, Nevada, in 1863. Nampa was a supply point for the Silver City mining area. (Courtesy, John Brandt)

gunsmoke settled, Koenig was mortally wounded.

Koenig was a "young, apparently well-liked man" and "many people were convinced that Dewey was a 'cold-blooded murderer' and should be punished." On October 2, 1884, a jury convicted Dewey of manslaughter and the judge sentenced him to "eight years at hard labor in the territorial prison at Boise." Dewey was incarcerated until March of 1885 when the territorial Supreme Court awarded him a new trial after a successful appeal to the body.

In May of 1885 a jury again reviewed the evidence surrounding the shoot-out. This time, Dewey rejoiced to hear, "We, the jury, find the defendant not guilty." The jury acquitted Dewey on the grounds of self-defense.

But the incident was not without consequences for Dewey. "The expenses of the trial plus the recession in mining caused by the failure of the Bank of California, left Dewey some $40,000 in debt and without credit --- his enemies had seen to that."

Dewey began the search for another profitable mine and by

After 1886, Dewey purchased and developed the Trade Dollar Mine in the Siver City area, shown here with the mining crew in a 1900 photo. Eventually he sold the mine for more than a million dollars. (ISHS)

the summer of 1886 he was in business again following the discovery of a rich gold vein in Florida Mountain. He went on to purchase and develop the Trade Dollar Mine which he eventually sold for more than a million dollars. He engaged in roadbuilding in Owyhee County and established the town of Dewey, three miles from Silver City, in 1896. According to his son, Con, his "grand, free-wheeling manner" earned him the nickname of "Colonel" at a stockholders meeting of the Trade Dollar mine at Frankfort, Kentucky.

Colonel Dewey is on the donkey at the center of this photo which was taken at the Thunder Mountain Mine in the Silver City area. (CCHS)

As Dewey began to age, he was not content to limit his influence to the mining districts of Owyhee County. He turned his attention to the Boise Valley, seeing a particular need for connecting Silver City to the main mode of transportation for the area, the Oregon Short Line.

Dewey began negotiations with Boise businessmen who, in turn, were still miffed over not being included on the main line of the Oregon Short Line railroad. They were anxious to have their own railroad and lessen their dependency on the "stub" line between Boise and Nampa.

Hoping to pressure the Oregon Short Line officials into building the railroad into Boise, a group of Boise businessmen made a deal with Colonel Dewey. They agreed to raise $300,000 and secure the right-of-way for a railroad line to the Owyhee mines which Dewey was to build. In addition, Boise was to donate a city block upon which Dewey agreed to build a $150,000 hotel.

After a handshake on the deal, Dewey journeyed East in the fall of 1895 to sell stock in his Silver City Trade Dollar Mine in order to finance the proposal. By the time he returned in the spring of 1896, the Boise businessmen had backed out of the venture. Angered, Dewey proclaimed, "I'll never do a thing for Boise as long as I live and I don't care if grass grows in the streets of Boise." He drove directly from Boise to Nampa. After conferring with various men, Dewey agreed to bail out the Townsite Company, build a railroad line to Owyhee County from Nampa and construct his hotel in Nampa. "Jilted" by Boise, some say that Colonel Dewey turned his attention to Nampa, "just for spite."

From 1896 until his death in 1903, Colonel Dewey spent most of his time in Nampa. In the fall of 1896, he began surveying for the Boise, Nampa and Owyhee railway which eventually ran thirty miles from Nampa to Murphy in Owyhee County. In 1897 he incorporated the Idaho Northern railroad and oversaw its construction as far as Emmett.

THE DEWEY PALACE

Then Dewey began his pet project. Initially, Dewey agreed to build a $35,000 hotel if Nampa would furnish the site. By June of 1900, the city had raised $3000 of the estimated $5500 to purchase the land and Dewey announced that "when the town had raised $4000, he would complete the balance." Also, by then, the Nampa City Council referred to the proposed structure as a $70,000 project.

Excavation for the basement began in 1900 and by February of 1901 the magnitude of the building was evident. The cost estimate for the 43,000 square foot structure was upped to $200,000. Built in the midst of sagebrush, the Dewey Palace rose "like a castle in a barren waste." The hotel was two hundred feet long by forty feet

W. H. Dewey died May 9, 1903 in his apartment in the recently completed Dewey Palace in Nampa. He is shown in this photo shortly before his death with his wife, Isabel Hagen Dewey, known as "Belle," and his daughter, Marie Dewey Davis. (ISHS)

Excavation for the basement of the Dewey Palace began in 1900. By the time the foundation of the building was laid, the mammoth size of the project was evident. (ISHS)

wide and took up most of a city block. Three stories in height, the structure contained double balconies along the front. The ceiling heights inside varied from eleven to twelve feet and the building contained an elevator. It was illuminated by both electric and gas lights.

Dewey left nothing out in his plans for the utilization of the space:

> For the basement, plans called for a billiard room, a bowling alley, four drummers' rooms, bathrooms, a barber shop, and storage space. On the main floor were the offices, the reading room, the parlor, the bar, the dining room, storage and pantries. On the second floor were the ballroom, a large parlor, a six-room 'ensuite' with baths, and some large bedrooms. The third story contained a four-room 'ensuite' and more bedrooms. The ballroom, usually called the assembly room, had a stage and removable seats.

Brick for Dewey's hotel was manufactured at the site. (Courtesy, Winston Goering)

Completed in December of 1902, the Dewey Palace cost approximately a quarter million dollars to construct. (ISHS)

The exterior of the building was stately. Dewey had a fondness for the pomp and elegance of Southern architecture, and so, on the desert ground of the Idaho West, he erected a mansion which could have come straight out of the deep South. The hotel displayed huge verandahs with carved columns. Gleaming copper sheeting covered two tower domes which stood above the roof line of the building. The structure was all brick.

Colonel Dewey ordered the carpets, linen and silver from Marshall-Field in Chicago and the furniture from Grand Rapids,

Containing approximately 43,000 square feet, the hotel was three stories in height and was serviced by its own electric power plant and water system. (ISHS)

The lobby of the Dewey Palace is shown here in the 1920s. (ISHS)

Colonel Dewey's son, E. H. Dewey, took over management of his father's business enterprises upon the Colonel's death. E. H. Dewey's office was in the Dewey Palace. (ISHS)

The dining room of the Dewey Palace was the scene of many an elegant social occasion. (ISHS)

The Dewey Palace bar was closed in 1910 when Canyon County went dry under a local option prohibition law. (ISHS)

Blanche Ruse, Alice Ayers and Carrie Findley, the owner, stand behind the counter in the candy shop and soda fountain of the Dewey Palace in 1918. (ISHS)

The bowling alley was located in the basement of the Dewey Palace. (CCHS)

Spare moments could be passed in the pool room of the Dewey hotel. (ISHS)

This 1923 photo shows the Twelfth Avenue side of the Dewey Palace. The hotel was 200 feet long by 40 feet wide, spanning the city block between Eleventh and Twelfth Avenues South. (ISHS)

Michigan. R. W. Purdum traveled to Pittsburgh to select an electrical light plant for the hotel. Charles Weiside, the hotel's first manager, brought twenty of the thirty assistants needed to operate the hotel with him from the East. W. K. Johnson of Chicago oversaw the project as the architect and J. M. Clark worked as construction engineer.

Completed in December of 1902, the Dewey Palace cost approximately a quarter million dollars to construct. Colonel Dewey moved in on December 31st and opened the hotel to the public on New Year's Day, 1903. Nampa and the surrounding valley celebrated the Grand Opening on February 20, 1903.

> Two special trains came from Boise, bringing dignitaries, the socialites and the curious. State legislators came almost en masse, along with the newly-inaugurated Governor Morrison of Caldwell and ex-Governor Hunt.

C. W. Mann, a telephone operator for Mountain States Telephone and Telegraph Company which was located in the Dewey Palace, drove his buggy to work everyday from his farm. (ISHS)

Other persons came from as far as San Francisco, Denver and Omaha.

Some estimated the crowd of visitors to be over two thousand people.

The hotel served a banquet beginning at eleven p.m. Friday evening and continuing in shifts of 140 to 150 each until the next morning. Nine hundred and twelve people feasted, free of charge, on "turkey, goose, chicken, guinea hen, consumme, nuts, raisins, and imported champagne." Dancing kept the place alive "until the tired musicians cased their instruments just in time to rush to the last train back to Boise at 4:30 a.m."

Dewey basked in the joy of his final accomplishment for only a few short months. On May 9, 1903, at the age of 79, he died, his obituary listing the cause of death as dropsy and liver complications. Dewey's son, E. H. Dewey, took over his father's business affairs.

The Dewey Palace exemplified the boldness of a man who took advantage of the untamed landscape of the West. Reckless, flamboyant, daring --- Colonel Dewey was not a conservative businessman. If he had been, the Dewey Palace would never have been built.

The furnishings of the hotel were sold at auction after the building was closed in 1956. (ISHS)

When Canyon County undertook to impose upon its citizens a more controlled environment, the Dewey Palace found itself in trouble. Because it would not maintain a profit in a county gone "dry" under prohibition, the Dewey Palace closed from March 9, 1912 to sometime in 1916. "Business has been poor ever since Nampa has been under prohibition rule," noted E. H. Dewey at the time of the closing. In fact, the hotel lost $89,700 prior to shutting the doors.

After serving for many years as a center of social and business functions for the city of Nampa, the Dewey Palace again fell on hard times in the 1950's. Closed in July of 1956 because it was no longer economically advantageous to manage the structure, the Dewey Palace was razed in 1963. The community has mourned ever since.

*The Dewey Palace was razed in 1963.
(Courtesy, Jerry Cornilles)*

BUSINESS BOOMS

Colonel Dewey was not the only person engaged in building new business enterprises in Nampa in the decade following the turn of the century. A cursory glance at the newspaper headlines during this decade tempts one to believe the Chamber of Commerce contention that Nampa was becoming "the Denver of Idaho." In the same vein, L. C. Van Riper, described by the Leader-Herald as a "prominent New York capitalist" who was moving to Nampa, challenged local residents to anticipate "that in ten years that instead of the modest estimate that some of you are putting on the population of 30,000 or 40,000 people, that you will have 200.000."

*This view of Nampa was taken in 1904.
(ISHS)*

When the Oregon Short Line depot was built in 1903, at least ten passenger trains arrived and departed daily from Nampa. (ISHS)

But in reality, Nampa's business community experienced a roller-coaster existence in the first decade of the twentieth century. Development either looked exceedingly good or gave cause for grave concern. The Nampa Leader-Herald during the summer and fall of 1906 heralded unprecedented growth for Nampa. In June of 1906 the paper announced that $150,000 worth of buildings were under construction in Nampa. New businesses promised for the area included an opera house, alfalfa meal plant, box factory, clothing store, grocery store, flour mill, saw mill, loan company, forwarding house, planning mill, dry goods store, International Harvester distributing house, sugar beet factory and brewery.

In October of 1906, the newspaper claimed that "as many as two hundred new buildings have been erected on our principal streets" during the last six months. Furthermore, the county assessor's records showed an increase of $95,667 on the valuation of Nampa property in September of 1906 as compared with the previous year. "This does not include the sugar beet factory, the brewery or the twenty new business houses in process of construction," the paper pointed out. "The future of Nampa never looked so good as it does today," the paper proclaimed.

The train depot displays a flurry of activity early in the twentieth century. (CCHS)

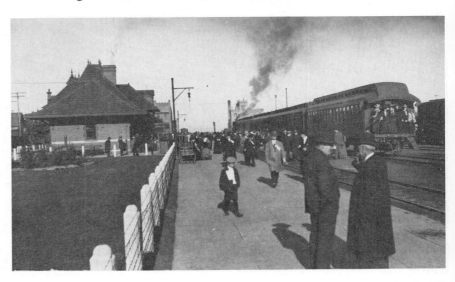

NAMPA'S FIRST SUGAR BEET FACTORY

Nampa succeeded in persuading two major industries to locate in the town during this time period, a beet factory, which came to the state out of Utah and incorporated as the Western Idaho Sugar Company, and the Crescent Brewing Company.

The sugar beet factory, actively solicited for the area by Nampa businessmen, became a surety once 5000 acres of beets were guaranteed by local farmers for processing at the plant. This goal was reached in June of 1905 and construction on the facility began that fall.

A $1,125,000 enterprise, the completed sugar beet plant contained 2,400,000 bricks, 400 tons of steel and 2000 tons of equipment. The construction work included the drilling of a 289 foot well, the completion of a water tank with a 95,000 gallon capacity, and the building of a 175 foot chimney which was put up at the rate of four feet per day and, in and of itself, required 375,000 bricks. The construction company paid wages of around $100,000 monthly during the building project.

Area farmers brought in 220 Japanese to help thin beets and prepare for the opening of the plant. By September of 1906, 1680 tons of beets were stockpiled at the factory. Operations began September 24, 1906. On this day, "a record-breaking 531 tons of

Sheep occupy the ground around the first sugar beet factory in this early photo. (ISHS)

Nampa's first sugar beet factory, constructed in 1905, is seen here with the sugar beet pond in the foreground. A $1,125,000 enterprise, the completed sugar beet plant contained 2,400,000 bricks, 400 tons of steel and 2000 tons of equipment. (ISHS)

By September of 1906, 1680 tons of beets were stockpiled at the sugar beet factory in anticipation of opening day. Operations began September 24, 1906. (ISHS)

beets were sliced instead of the average 200 ton first-day-run." The first season closed December 3, 1906. During the fall the company processed 41,000 tons of beets, paid $60,000 in wages, and bought $200,000 worth of beets from the farmers. The enterprise was considered a success.

Most Nampa citizens heralded the construction of the sugar beet plant as a major step forward for the Nampa business and farming communities; however, the factory did cause some conflict in town. One of Nampa's founders, J. A. McGee, threatened to move to Weiser because the new sugar factory was built by Mormons, or members of the Church of Jesus Christ of Latter Day Saints. In a newspaper story headlined, "Fleeing From the Mormons," the Leader-Herald announced that if it had to make a choice between McGee and the new industry, "We take the sugar factory." The paper decried the fact that McGee was knocking the town, but ascribed his actions to "one of his vagaries." Evidently McGee's threat was idle, for in December of 1907 the newspaper reported that he was still in town.

The Western Idaho Sugar Company consolidated with the Utah Sugar Company and the Idaho Sugar Company before the beginning of the 1907 season. The newly formed Utah-Idaho Sugar Company carried a capital of $10,000,000 in preferred stock and $3,000,000 in common stock. Production figures would lead one to believe that the 1907 season continued the success story of the first year. In sixty days, the plant processed 48,000 tons and paid $300,000 for labor and beets.

However, during this season, troubling incidents forecast the eventual demise of the company. A tight money market made it difficult to secure currency for the payroll. Japanese laborers caused trouble when low yield per acre cut the basis for their wages. Also, area farmers claimed the company was responsible for furnishing seed which produced a small beet, rich in sugar content, but inadequate in size to yield tonnage sufficient to make a profit. Overall, even though the farmers contracted with the plant for almost double the acreage of the first season, the final yield was increased

Nampa's first sugar beet factory operated only until 1910. In 1915, the factory was dismantled and the equipment was sent to Spanish Fork, Utah. Two years later, the Carnation Company milk condensery located at the site which was purchased for them by Nampa businessmen for $5000. The original brick chimney stood until it was pulled down in January of 1980. (ISHS, donated by the Idaho Statesman)

by less than twenty percent. Some disgruntled farmers refused to sign up for another year.

In 1908 the beet crop was good but the acreage was small. Most of the crop came to Nampa from other localities. The company threatened to move. In 1909 blight wiped out the limited acreage that was planted in sugar beets and the plant did not open for the fall campaign. In 1910 rain and the white fly damaged the limited crop. The plant opened, but the processing lasted only eleven days.

The plant stood idle in 1911 and 1912. Farmers, unable to make a profit, refused to gamble on growing sugar beets. In November of 1912, Thomas C. Cutler, the general manager of the Utah-Idaho Sugar Company, announced that the plant would definitely be moved. In 1915 two hundred workers dismantled the factory and sent the machinery to Spanish Fork, Utah.

THE CRESCENT BREWING COMPANY

The newly organized Nampa Chamber of Commerce distributed thousands of pamphlets advertising the town at the Portland Exposition in 1905. In response to this appeal, Jacob Lockman contacted the Chamber in November of that year regarding the possibility of constructing a brewery in Nampa. The Chamber reacted positively, agreeing to furnish a site for the business.

In January of 1906 Jacob and Freda Lockman moved to Nampa from Wallace, Idaho where Jacob had been mayor of the town. Both of the Lockmans migrated to this country from Germany as youngsters, Jacob when he was fourteen and Freda when she was eight.

As they began making plans for the establishment of the Crescent Brewing Company, Jacob Lockman sent to Chicago for Bernard Barthel, an architect and engineer who specialized in the building of breweries, malt houses and industrial plants, to design the structure. Pat Murphy was the contractor for the project.

By the time construction was completed, Nampa was indeed proud of the new business. The newspaper called the $130,000 building "mammoth." The main structure varied in height from one to four stories and contained approximately 24,500 square feet. The portion of the brewery housing the bottling works added another 3200 square feet. The Lockmans special-ordered a million bricks which were used for the exterior of the building. Concrete covered the floors "except in the cellar and ice-house where cork was used."

The plant started operation in January of 1907 and continued brewing "Overland" beer until it began fighting the battles of prohibition a couple of years later. In August of 1909 Canyon County's "Drys" prevailed in a local option election by a vote of 3162 for prohibition to 1308 against. Nampa, however, disagreed with the majority, but to no avail. The only place in the county to oppose prohibition, Nampa voted 537 to retain the status quo to 517 to go dry.

When a Moscow, Idaho district court judge ruled that "near-beer" violated the local option law, the Nampa Leader-Herald reacted with the following:

Jacob P. Lockman moved to Nampa from Wallace, Idaho in January of 1906 and founded the Crescent Brewing Company in 1907. (Courtesy, W. Lockman)

It is almost too much --- it's the limit, also the last straw. It might almost be called down-right cruelty, and is governed by the same sublime reasoning that caused the canine to loose his caudal appendage a little at a time in order to reduce his suffering to a minimum.

On the basis of this decision, Sheriff Breshears and County Attorney Hagelin notified the Crescent Brewery not to sell any more Landover near-beer to dealers or individuals. Six "near-beer 'joints'" were also affected in Nampa --- the Cosmopolitan, Commercial, Pullman, Capital, Dewey Palace and Nampa bars.

For the purpose of testing the law, Jacob Lockman sold two bottles of near-beer to Deputy Sheriff Paynter. Although a chemist testified at the preliminary hearing in Caldwell that "it would be impossible for a person to drink enough near-beer to become intoxicated," Lockman was bound over to district court and placed under a $500 bond. The defendant refused to pay bail but "while he was supposedly in jail to comply with the order of the court, Mr. Lockman was not confined there but allowed perfect freedom."

Located on Ninth Avenue North, the Crescent Brewery brewed "Overland" beer until the plant was converted in 1915 to a factory for the production of soft drinks, cider and grape juice. When prohibition was repealed in 1933, the enterprise returned to the brewing business. (Courtesy, Jerry Cornilles)

In August of 1910 the Idaho Supreme Court ruled against Lockman and the Crescent Brewery. The local paper reported:

The court holds that it is not necessary to show that the beverage is intoxicating. The law mentions malt liquors, among others, as being prohibited and it is freely admitted that Near Beer is a malt liquor, although chemical analysis showed that it contains but 1.28 per cent alcohol and is therefore non-intoxicating.

Obviously feeling that the decision was overly strict, the Leader-Herald fretted that "about everything but pure water may be prohibited." In an editorial critical of the decision, the newspaper concluded: "If carried out to the strict letter all tonics, cordials, extracts and essences can be put under the ban, for they are mixtures containing intoxicating liquor."

When in May of 1913 the Idaho Supreme Court again went against the brewery and decided that beer could not be shipped from a railroad terminus in a dry territory to a wet area, in this case, McCall, Idaho, the fate of the Crescent Brewery Company was clear. Converted in 1915 to a factory for the production of soft drinks, cider and grape juice, the plant, now called "The Overland Beverage Company," met the demands of the statewide prohibition law which went into effect on January 1, 1916.

Operation of the plant as a soft-drink factory proved to be a successful venture. However, when prohibition was repealed in 1933, the Lockmans returned to the brewing business. Machinery arrived from Germany and Charles Inderweis, the brewmaster, supervised its installation.

The brewery continued operating until the mid-1940s when competition with large companies forced numerous small brewery enterprises out of business. Most of the machinery was sent to Bogota, Colombia, South America, including the 14,000-pound copper kettle which was used for brewing the beer. Because the kettle was twelve feet in diameter, a fourteen foot hole had to be knocked out of the side of the building in order to remove the kettle and load it on a railroad flat car.

The main structure stood vacant from 1953 until 1966 when its current owner, Julius Kleiner, ordered it razed. The bottle house, which was adjacent to the main complex, still stands as does the home which the Lockmans built beside their enterprise.

The Jacob Lockman residence, built in 1903 next to the brewery, still stands. (ISHS)

BUSINESS FALLS ON HARD TIMES

The sugar beet factory and the brewery exemplify that all was not smooth sailing for enterprises begun during the years of ambition following the turn of the century. Even at the time, at least one Nampa resident was skeptical of the "boom" atmosphere of 1906.

F. G. Cottingham found that "Nampa has been one of the most widely advertised towns in the state" and yet everything that was promised did not come to pass. "If you will rake over this

This 1902 photo of downtown Nampa shows the muddy streets and wooden boardwalks which were evident in the business district of town. (ISHS)

scrap heap, there will be work for your thinker if it is in repair," he said.

> By lengthy articles in our paper we have been informed that Nampa was going to have the following: A pickle plant, farm machinery factory, and a soap factory; in its time there was a pottery establishment, but after a time [it] died. Then at various times there was announced that we were going to have a scouring plant, a sash and door factory, a broom factory, a vinegar and mustard works

And that wasn't all.

> A Colorado man was going to put up a portable house plant, a $50,000 theater, not the present one, a military academy; another announced that Hibbard Spencer and Bartlett were going to build a large warehouse. A waterlifting factory was established but failed, and an evaporator that was started and stopped; add to these two steam railroads and two electric lines that there has been time and money spent upon, that have not materialized, yet these reaching to a point not now connected leads us to think that Nampa is an easy mark for dreamers.

Maybe "dreamers" was too complimentary a term, continued Cottingham, "Maybe I should have used the word suckers." He gave this example:

> A fellow comes along -- he was just another -- and asked us to help him and he would build us a fine Opery house. Well about forty of us gave him $25.00 a piece; 'Oh! sure I will pay you all back in just a little while.' All we ever got was a ticket to the opening show. But maybe we should not complain for that was the starter of the Majestic, now a very fine show place.

This theater was built in 1910 by R. E. Elvers at a cost of nearly $20,000. Vaudeville shows played here for many years and in the late 1920s sound movies were presented. The theater later became the Fox Majestic and operated until 1958 when it was destroyed by fire. (Courtesy, Jerry Cornilles)

Within a year of the "boom" of 1906, Nampa's growth had slowed considerably. In November of 1907 the Nampa Leader-Herald tried to stir the loyal residents out of the "pessimism." "Many people in Nampa complain about what they term the 'quietude' of the town and bitterly compare the present condition with that of last year when the town was enjoying a boom," the paper pointed out. The sugar beet factory had closed for the season and the saw mill, too, had shut down, taking away "a good portion of the city's payroll." However, the article claimed "Nampa is going ahead every day, probably not so fast, nor with as much a hurrah as last year but nevertheless going ahead."

By 1908 Nampa business was clearly in a slump. The Leader-Herald carried several stories of business failures. In January a credit association took over the Nampa Mercantile Company because of "financial troubles which have been brewing for some time past." Liquidation of the stock and collections on accounts payable took place in order to pay off the indebtedness. The newspaper praised the store for carrying "splendid stock" and being "square dealing in every sense of the word" and regretted "the unfortunate turn of affairs."

Within a few days the paper reported financial trouble for the New York Store. After being closed for several days, this store hoped to pull out of its difficulties by having a "big money raising sale."

The Nampa Times, a forerunner to the Nampa Leader-Herald, was started in 1888. This 1902 photo shows the offices of the newspaper when they were located at Eleventh Avenue and 1st Street South. (ISHS)

The interior of this early newspaper office is shown around the turn of the century. This enterprise was located in the 200 block of Twelfth Avenue South. (ISHS)

The Bon Ton Bakery was owned by Mr. and Mrs. Oscar Bauman, shown here in the interior of the store with their son in October of 1908. (ISHS)

The Union Grocery Company, shown here before the 1909 fire, was located at 1217 Main Street. (ISHS)

Harold Stewart is shown in the New York Market delivery wagon with the horse, Old Fat, in this 1914 photo. (ISHS)

Frank Huntley stands at the counter inside the Huntley Grocery. (CCHS)

The Falk Bloch Mercantile Company, Limited, located between Tenth and Eleventh Avenues on Front Street, was one of two general stores in Nampa which supplied the needs of the community at the turn of the century. The store opened in this area shortly after the establishment of the town. (CCHS)

Ed Saunders, Alvera LaRue, Mr. Gaudy and Cloed Duval stand inside the Falk store when it was located on Twelfth Avenue and First Street South. Currently, this building houses Kalbus Office Supply. (CCHS)

The Falk Mercantile Company is shown here after it moved to the corner of Twelfth Avenue and First Street South. (CCHS)

Dr. Frank Hostetler, an early Nampa veterinarian, practiced in town from 1905 to 1955. (ISHS)

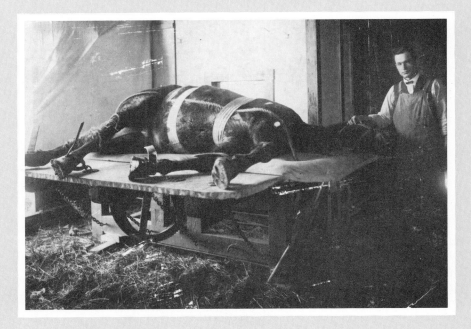

The Hatfield Harness and Saddle Shop was located on Main Street, later called First Street. (Courtesy, Lucy Redmon)

Early in the century, Wylie Oliver ran a popcorn stand on the corner of Twelfth Avenue and Main Street. Later, he moved his stand to the corner of the Dewey Palace grounds at Eleventh Avenue and Main Street. (ISHS)

The Brandt Brothers Building was constructed in 1909 between Tenth and Eleventh Avenues on First Street. (Courtesy, John Brandt)

The Red Front Store and Second Hand Bargain House was located on Front Street in Nampa in the early 1900s. L. M. Lisonbee, the owner of the store, is standing in front of his shop with an unidentified woman. (ISHS)

About a week later, the Nampa Wall Paper and Paint Company announced that its manager, George C. Parsons, quietly slipped out of town with his wife and child, "their destination being unknown and unheralded." Parsons left two partners "holding the sack, and left a number of unpaid bills about the city." The partners accused Parsons of appropriating money from the business for his own personal use.

Harry Robb, a Nampa clothing store proprietor, summed up the feeling of the town. "Every ten minutes of the day you hear about so and so being in hard shape, about this and that institution being up against it," he said. He was not sympathetic to the business failures, however. "Not one single failure here has been caused by the existing conditions," he claimed, but instead he blamed incompetent management and deceptive retail practices for the financial woes.

The financial condition of Nampa's business community became the primary consideration when the city proposed a paving program for Nampa's streets in February of 1908. A considerable number of residents circulated and presented to city council a petition opposing the civic improvement project. "In view of the condition in financial circles and the consequent tightness of money" this group argued that the work should be deferred. Those proposing the paving plan agreed that money was tight in Nampa, but thought that proceeding with the project would "give work to many idle men, thereby distributing money among the merchants of the city."

The proponents won out. The city opted to go ahead with the paving project even though a special election yielded a "decided majority" opposing the proposition. The city reasoned that the public improvements would help provide much needed work to Nampa's laboring men at a time when "there has been very little work the last few months." "The harder the times the more important and imperative is our duty to provide what we can for the bone and sinew of our community," they thought.

A year later, business again took a turn for the better in Nampa. By the spring and summer of 1909 once again, the newspaper bragged on the new and enlarged commercial developments being undertaken. The paper announced plans for building an opera house and for the enlargement of the quarters of the Conley Lumber Company, the Nampa Department Store and the Roberts Dry Goods Company.

Trade on the Oregon Short Line and the Idaho Northern was up substantially as was trade in general at most of Nampa's stores. The hotel proprietors often boasted of full houses, the real estate men reported a decided increase in sales, and the construction industry announced a demand for new houses.

Assuring the public that it was not writing "a 'boom' article in the common sense of the word -- the hot-air effusion of a booster with a reckless disregard for truth," the Leader-Herald proclaimed that "business of the city [is] almost double what it was for the same period of last year."

THE FIRE OF 1909

Preparations for Nampa's Fourth of July celebration in 1909 began as early as April. "This is Nampa's year to have a hummer," the newspaper announced.

By June, the town was ready to honor the holiday with "the biggest celebration ever held in southern Idaho." The "regular program" of music, dancing, baseball, races and sports was to be supplemented by a rock drilling contest of special interest to miners,

On Saturday afternoon, July 3, 1909, a stranger entered the Arnold cigar store and ignited a fireworks display which started one of the worst fires in Nampa's history. (ISHS)

The 1909 fire started in the store at the far left corner of the block shown in this picture. (ISHS)

a parade, and a traditional patriotic speech by Judge C. F. Malsberry of Cincinnati, "a most eloquent speaker." The town ordered five hundred dollars of fireworks which were on their way from New York. The committee scheduled the program and activities to "take the entire day without a moment of 'nothing doing.'"

But the fireworks went off early. At about three o'clock on Saturday afternoon, July 3rd, a fairly well-dressed stranger entered the Arnold cigar store. Looking over a display of fireworks, he picked up a "bomb," inquired as to its price, and then remarked that he would "see how it would burn." In a surprising, irrational move, the stranger "applied the match." Before Mr. Arnold could throw the "bomb" out, it exploded in his hands, setting off the other fireworks. "Everything seemed to burst into a blaze all at once," the paper reported. The three or four horrified witnesses in the store escaped through the open front door, as did the stranger, never to be seen again.

The stranger's actions seemed to be without motivation. Some speculated that he was a tramp, since the cigar store was close to the train depot and tracks. "The report on the streets was that the man was drunk or crazy," but Mr. Arnold and his partner didn't think so. They attributed his actions to a case of "pure cussedness."

Within three hours, the fire completely demolished twenty-five

About half of the business district of Nampa was destroyed in the 1909 fire, including Nampa's first financial institution, the Bank of Nampa. (ISHS)

stores and "burned out" sixty businesses. "Not a single building was left on the entire block bounded by Front and First streets and Twelfth and Thirteenth Avenues," this area comprising about half of the business district of Nampa.

The catastrophe caused considerable damage to businesses in the neighboring blocks. The heat scorched buildings, broke out windows and damaged awnings. The fire even threatened the Dewey Palace when the wind blew flying embers onto its roof. Men stationed on the roof and the verandahs waited with pails of water or hoses attached to water pipes inside the hotel and put out each new blaze before it got a good start.

When the fire was about to be brought under control, a barrel of oil in the Bowman Paint and Oil Store exploded. No one was injured but "about half the people in town went absolutely crazy," recalled Fred. G. Mock, a spectator to the event.

Within three hours, the 1909 fire completely demolished twenty-five stores and burned out sixty businesses, destroying the entire block between Front and First Streets and Twelfth and Thirteenth Avenues. (ISHS)

Business men whose stores faced that burned block, commenced to pile their goods out on the sidewalks; men ran here and there, left musical instruments, show cases of jewelry, clothing, dry goods, and such, and carried potatoes, onions, turnips, corn and what have you, from a grocery store . . . around to the vacant lots where the United Presbyterian Church now stands.

The attempt to save merchandise and furnishings from threatened businesses resulted in additional damage. Mock described the scene:

Frank Rockwell and George Mayhew stand with the horses in Nampa's fire station in approximately 1912. (Courtesy, Lucy Redmon)

By 1913 or 1914, Frank Rockwell and George Mayhew were driving Nampa's first fire truck, a 1910 "White". Archie Taylor is on the side of the fire engine. This photo was taken on the corner of Eleventh Avenue and Second Street South. (ISHS)

"Now, the firestation was the old Nampa Community Center. It's kitty-corner across from the firestation today. I would stay there for hours, waiting for a fire so that I could see the horses. They had the harnesses hanging from the ceiling. Now the horses were stabled in the back. If the fire siren went off --- the horses were never tied --- but they would back out of their stalls. The harnesses [were] suspended from the ceiling. [The horses] would back into their positions on the fire wagon and they would drop the harnesses on their back, hook the belly button, or the belly bands, and the collars. I never ever got to see the horses take off on a file."

---Elmer Burri

This fire station was built in 1910 on First Street South and served the city until it was replaced in 1957. At that time it was remodeled into a Community Center. (ISHS)

By 1926, Nampa had three fire trucks, including this one. (NPL)

Nampa businesses lost more than $300,000 in the 1909 fire. Most merchants had insufficient insurance to cover their losses. For example, J. N. Brunzell, owner of the Grand Hotel shown here, estimated his loss at about $30,000 but carried only $8000 in insurance. (ISHS)

Those who kept their wits about them, carried and helped with valuable goods, but when they came to a pile of goods a block or so away, they threw what they had brought on the pile and ran back for another load. It was almost a week before merchants found their goods and got things straightened out.

Perhaps the entire business district would have been lost had it not been for the Boise and Caldwell fire departments. When Nampa's volunteers began fighting the fire, "the hose was coupled up and water turned on" but "there was no pressure." In changing from wooden to iron pipes, disconnections had been made, rendering the system useless.

"For the next half hour practically nothing was done" but within an hour the Boise fire department arrived with a "big steamer and hook and ladder outfit." After receiving a call for help, the Boise people loaded their equipment onto a special train and "made the run to Nampa, a distance of twenty miles, in eighteen minutes." Caldwell also answered the call for assistance and arrived promptly with an auto filled with "a long string of hose" which was badly needed.

Ironically, on July first, Nampa had approved a bond issue

Many businesses announced new locations and opened to the public within a week after the 1909 fire. (ISHS)

by a vote of 213 to 39 taxing itself $20,000 "to be used for the maintenance and equipment of a fire department" including a new fire engine "steamer."

When the unscrupulous few began pilfering, Mayor E. H. Dewey deputized twenty-five special policemen, "armed them with revolvers and gave instructions to shoot any one caught stealing, and shoot to kill." The mayor also ordered the saloons closed at nine that evening in order "to avoid any danger of trouble on the part of those who were inclined to indulge too freely in intoxicants after the fire."

After the smoke settled, loss to Nampa businesses was extensive, running to more than $300,000. Most merchants had some insurance, but insufficient to cover their losses and rebuilding costs. J. N. Brunzell, for example, owner of the Grand Hotel and some other businesses, estimated his loss at about $30,000 but carried only $8000 in insurance. That did not defeat him, however. Within a few days he had "put up a temporary frame structure" on the burned out property on Front street and had reopened his saloon "in order to use his unexpired license."

Many businesses announced new locations and opened to the public within a week. The Nampa Record went so far as to set up headquarters in a tent at the rear of the Leader-Herald building so as not to miss publication of a single issue. They shared the Leader-Herald machinery in order to print their newspaper.

Much was made of the fact that the Fourth of July celebration went on as planned, minus the fireworks display. The parade included a group of businessmen who called themselves the "Cinder Club." They carried banners bearing inscriptions appropriate to the occasion, including: "My Contract is Let," "More Brick for Nampa," "Gone Up in Smoke But Have Not Lost Hope," and "Burned But Not Busted."

At least two Chinese businessmen, one the owner of a laundry, paraded as part of the "Cinder Club," carrying the following placards: "Washee Allee Samee" and "Me No Likee Firee."

This is the corner of First Street and Twelfth Avenue South following the 1909 fire. (Courtesy, Winston Goering)

III
Life in Nampa:
1910 - 1917

The census at the turn of the century gave Nampa a population of 799. Ten years later, the town had increased to 4205, a growth rate four times more rapid than the state as a whole and nearly twice as rapid as the rest of Canyon County.

Nationally, business analysts thought the year 1910 to be disturbing and disappointing for American finance and industry. Yet in Nampa business development continued at the beginning of the new decade. Much of the construction taking place in town was due to the rebuilding that took place following the 1909 fire. Once this work was completed, however, building activity shifted mainly to the construction of homes. In April of 1910 Inspector Reinhardt of the city issued building permits totaling $48,050 which included permits for ten homes valued at $2000 or less and a permit for a new Catholic Church valued at $20,000.

But in that same month a more significant event took place in Nampa, an event that in turn would have major impact upon the business community of the town. April 1, 1910 saw the closing of

Eleventh Avenue South crosses First Street South in this 1914 photo of downtown Nampa which was taken looking north from the top of the city water tank in 1914. The vacant corner lot with the sign is the present location of the Nampa Public Library. (ISHS)

Facing page: Nampa's train depot, shown here around 1915, was a focal point for much of the activity in town during the early decades of the twentieth century. (CCHS)

Numerous businesses in downtown Nampa are seen by looking east from the top of the city water tank in 1914. (ISHS)

This picture, taken in 1914 from the city water tank looking northwest toward Caldwell, shows the Presbyterian church and rectory located between Second and Third Streets South. (ISHS)

the saloons in Nampa as a result of the local option law which was voted into effect by the citizens of Canyon County in August of 1909.

NAMPA REACTS TO PROHIBITION

Life before the days of prohibition is reenacted in this photo taken in 1926 in a local pool hall. The town's businessmen staged the scene to help celebrate the opening of the P.F.E. shops in Nampa. (ISHS)

Larry Maloney served as chief of police in Nampa for almost twenty years, from 1904 to 1923. He was police chief during the early days of prohibition and was responsible for enforcing the local option law. In 1923, the day after Eugene Emerson was elected mayor, Maloney walked into his office and laid down his badge and baton. "I suppose you want these," he said. "Yes," replied Emerson, "that's what the campaign was all about." Nampa was supposedly notorious for its pool halls. (CCHS)

The Nampa Leader-Herald reported that Nampa's bars, the Cosmopolitan, the Grand and the Commercial bar, "did a good business" on their final day with "the rush" for liquor continuing until the closing of the doors at midnight. "Not only was there considerable liquor dished up by the genial barkeepers for immediate consumption at the bar, but many citizens laid in a supply for future reference, for use in case the drouth proves to be too strenuous," the newspaper observed.

Two of the proprietors of Nampa's saloons, Antone Hinkey and W.J. Weaver, announced that their business establishments would remain open each to be operated as a soft drink and cigar store. J.M. Brunzell, owner of the Grand bar located in the Dewey building, announced that his place of business would be closed and that in all probability the room it occupied would be rented as a restaurant.

Within two weeks, by April 12th, Police Chief Larry Maloney made the first arrests for the illegal consumption of alcoholic beverages in town. When a number of men were seen "hanging around" without "any particular business," Maloney and his force became suspicious. "Watch was kept on them and along about 5 o'clock it was decided that it would be better for the community to have them where it would not be so much trouble to keep an eye on them," the newspaper reported. When the police force rounded up the men, the officers found a bottle of alcohol and "it was quite evident that all had sampled the contents more or less." The men refused to tell where they got the "tanglefoot." Judge Hart sentenced

CHIEF OF POLICE
LARRY MALONEY

The Pullman Bar is shown after prohibition went into effect in Nampa in 1910. The bar sold cigars, candy and fountain drinks but kept the bar decor. (CCHS)

four of the "ringleaders" to ten days in jail and sent the other six out of town.

Within the next couple of weeks, the county attorney, Fred Hagelin, made the first arrests in Nampa for "bootlegging." Antone Hinkey, former saloon keeper, Walter Sterk and Roy Waltman faced charges of selling liquor. Although the Nampa Leader-Herald editorialized on the day that prohibition went into effect in the town that "there should be no need of law and order leagues," the authorities arrested these Nampa businessmen after evidence was procured against them by members of Boise's Law and Order League.

When the three Nampa men came to court for their preliminary hearings a few days after their arrests, spectators crowded the courtroom. Johnson McNichols, the "star witness", testified first against Hinkey. He stated that on the 28th of April he went into the Commercial bar which Hinkey ran and asked for some whiskey. According to McNichols' testimoney, Hinkey went to a back room and returned with a half pint of the prohibited drink.

Defendant Hinkey, represented in court by Attorney Estabrook, denied ever seeing his accuser outside of the courtroom. Furthermore, Estabrook put two men on the stand who testified that McNichols' "reputation for truth and veracity was generally speaking, very bad." Then Estabrook "caused quite a sensation in the courtroom" by asking McNichols if he had a gun. When he admitted that he did, Police Chief Maloney placed the Law and Order detective under arrest for carrying a concealed weapon. After this dramatic turn of events, Justice Estes dismissed the case.

Walter Sterk did not fare as well as Hinkey. He represented himself and tried to establish an alibi concerning his whereabouts at the time that McNichols accused him of selling liquor. The judge failed to buy his story and bound him over to district court for trial.

By the time Roy Waltman took the stand, the newspaper reporter, for one, felt that McNichols, the star witness, had been thoroughly discredited. The reporter noted:

Whether it was because McNichols had lost his nerve when he had his big gun taken from him, had been under the strain of carrying the bottled evidence too long without sampling the same, or had been able to learn from remarks made by several of those present that men of his calibre were not held in much favor here, . . . his evidence on this case was contradictory all the way through.

Attorney Lamson, representing Waltman, portrayed the defendant as "a good citizen of splendid reputation in the community with too much business and too much respect for himself to engage in bootlegging whiskey at 35 cents per bottle." Justice Estes also dismissed the case against Waltman.

Nampa's police force, including the first motorcycle policeman, is shown in approximately 1917. (CCHS)

The town's reaction to this hearing made it clear that aggressive monitoring of the prohibition law by citizens' groups was not welcomed in Nampa. The Leader-Herald was highly critical of the Law and Order League in an editorial a few days after the hearing. The paper thought that the local police officers were doing a good job enforcing prohibition and that the interference of the Law and Order League only turned the question of enforcement into a "fiasco."

Less than ten months after prohibition went into effect in Nampa, business conditions in the town were disastrous. The town suffered from "a financial depression, depreciation of property valuations and injury to commercial enterprises," according to the Nampa Leader-Herald, mainly because of the enactment of the local option law.

The situation was so severe that the Chamber of Commerce called a meeting of representative businessmen. With "over sixty of the most prominent energetic business and professional men of the city" attending, the group unanimously endorsed a proposal to secede from Canyon County and join the County of Ada which had not yet enacted a local option law. R.M. Purdum, former mayor; S.D. McLain of the Stoddard Hardware company; V.T. Elver of the Elver Clothing company; Jacob Lockman of the Crescent Brewery;

Harry Robb of the Robb Clothing store; Attorney Frank Estabrook, Sr.; Otto Reinhardt, former Canyon County commissioner; and Mayor E.H. Dewey all spoke in favor of the proposition.

These and others expressed the general sentiment that Nampa had nothing in common with the rest of the county and that "it would be impossible for Nampa by any kind of a change to get a worse deal than it is now getting at the hands of Canyon County." Estabrook, known as "one of the most bitter of the many anti-local-option advocates" emphasized "the depressing effects of local option on local business" and commented that prohibition "had been forced on the people of Nampa by the rest of the county against their will and sentiment." He also thought that prejudice was rampant against Nampa in the rest of the county.

The group unanimously passed a resolution favoring the annexation of Nampa to Ada County and pledged to do all in its power to fulfill this goal. One month later the state legislature dashed any hopes Nampa businessmen had of rearranging county lines. When Nampa's annexation bill reached the floor of the House of Representatives, the legislators received it without favor. Ignoring a petition "bearing about 90 per cent of the names of the voters in the affected territory," the House indefinitely postponed the measure, dealing the bill its death blow.

When attempts to join Ada County failed, Nampans turned to another avenue to try to relieve the depression experienced in the town. In July of 1911 the "Anti-Local Option Association of Canyon County" organized and began a campaign to defeat the local option law. In the next few months the county saw "the hottest campaign in its entire history."

Those favoring the defeat of the local option law drew the issue in terms of the regulated and licensed saloon versus the bootlegger. Prohibition had not stopped the consumption of alcoholic beverages, they claimed, but had only "bred lawlessness and contempt for law and made law breakers of otherwise law-abiding citizens." During the previous two years when Nampa was under the local option law, "just as much liquor has been drank," the opponents of the law argued. "The only difference is that it has been just a little more difficult and expensive to get."

Furthermore, county option had been disastrous to business, said those wishing to repeal the law. In an article written for the Nampa Leader-Herald, A. E. Blunck contended that when

Less than ten months after prohibition went into effect in Nampa, business conditions in the town were disastrous. Consequently, over sixty businessmen, including V. T. Elver of the Elver Clothing Company shown in this 1913-1914 photo, unanimously voted to request the state legislature to allow Nampa to join Ada County which had not yet enacted a local option law. (CCHS)

Sept 5/11

Harry Robb of the Robb Clothing store was among those who wanted Nampa to secede from Canyon County in 1911. Robb was known for his innovative advertising and aggressive business practices. (ISHS)

prohibition went into effect in the county, "there was hardly a vacant house or store in the city." Two years later, "there are at least a hundred vacant houses and a number of stores, most of the latter vacated through failures." In addition, "not a single family has moved in because Nampa was a dry town, but . . . good people have passed on to other places because of that fact."

In an intense and forthright campaign, the opponents of prohibition in the county called theirs the only "sane" position. Convinced that "financial distress and prospective ruin" would continue to haunt Nampa businesses, the "wet" forces said Boise was the only one to profit from Canyon County's local option law. "Thousands and thousands of dollars have gone out of Nampa and other thousands have not come here that otherwise would, had there been the regulated saloon," the Leader-Herald editorialized the day before the election.

When the votes were cast in September of 1911, the voter turn-out demonstrated the intensity of the campaign. Nearly twice as many people cast ballots as two years earlier --- 8648 as compared with 4470 in 1909 --- yet the results remained the same. Canyon County's citizens mandated the continuation of the local option law by a 2412 vote majority.

However, Nampa continued to show its disagreement with the rest of the county. The "wet" forces prevailed in the three Nampa precincts. Out of 1723 votes cast in Nampa, there were 1090 people voting against county-wide prohibition or 63% of the vote cast, as compared with 633 who supported the local option law or 37% of those voting. This gave a "wet" majority of 457 votes as compared with 25 votes in 1909.

Business conditions in Nampa did not improve. The Dewey Palace exemplified the impact of the county prohibition law on commercial enterprises in Nampa. One Nampa citizen said it resembled "a summer resort hotel in October." By March of 1912, Nampa's pride and joy closed completely, citing its inability to compete with hotels in Boise which could still serve liquor. It reopened only after statewide prohibition went into effect, leveling out conditions between Canyon County and neighboring Ada County.

Also, bootlegging continued in the town. In September of 1913, Antone Hinkey once again was taken into custody after his "soft drink joint" was searched and seven jugs of whiskey were found in the basement. This time he was charged with "maintaining a nuisance."

This early photo shows the Bank of Nampa, the town's first financial institution, before it relocated in the block which was destroyed in the 1909 fire. This building was also occupied by the Boise and Nampa Irrigation and Power Company. (ISHS)

FINANCIAL WOES: THE BANK OF NAMPA FAILS

On September 27, 1913 the severity of the business depression in Nampa became evident when the Bank of Nampa, Nampa's oldest financial establishment, failed to open its doors. On that Saturday morning, at 10 a.m. when the bank would have normally opened, patrons found the following notice posted in the window: "This institution is in the hands of the bank commissioner." The newspaper called the bank closure "the sensation of the year."

The action came after an examination by Deputy Bank Commissioner A. A. Record who reportedly found the bank's reserve fund to be below the legal limit. The bank claimed a capitalization of $100,000 and deposits totaling $290,000 at the time of the bank failure.

The Leader-Herald reported that although no official statement had yet been issued, the bank failed because "the present depression in realty values" made it impossible to collect on long term loans. Also, the "losses sustained by the bank" in the 1909 fire had a

The Bank of Nampa was rebuilt after the 1909 fire in the same location where the building burned, the corner of Twelfth Avenue and First Street South. The bank was located there until it closed in September of 1913. The losses suffered by the bank in the 1909 fire had a bearing on the inability of the bank to remain viable. (ISHS)

bearing on the inability of the bank to remain viable.

The bank closure caused "considerable apprehension" to Nampans, but the newspaper assured its readers that there was no cause for alarm to those having deposits in Nampa's other two banking establishments, the Citizens State Bank and the First National Bank. In fact, E. H. Dewey, as administrator of the Dewey estate, took upon himself the responsibility of personally guaranteeing the deposits in Nampa's other two banks.

The Bank of Nampa had been founded in 1901 by Fred G. Mock. C. R. Hickey acquired a half interest in the business a year later and in 1905 it became a state bank with a capital of $50,000. In 1907 Dr. J. W. Givens of Orofino purchased the controlling interest and his son, J. A. Givens was vice president and manager of the bank at the time of its closure.

In an editorial three days after the bank failure, the Leader-Herald made no pretense as to the seriousness of the situation. It noted that the bank closure was probably the "most

This cashier's check shows bank script issued by the Bank of Nampa for ten dollars. (ISHS)

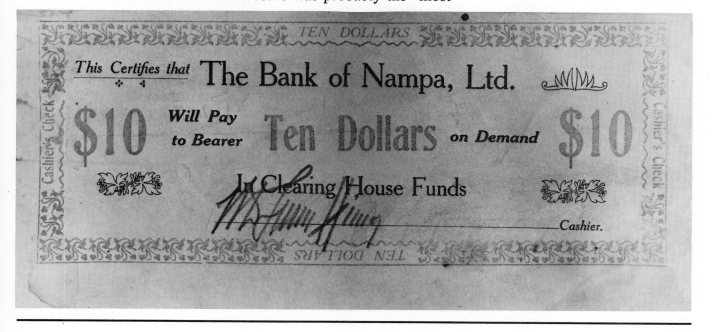

severe" blow that had happened to Nampa up to that time and that because of the closure, business conditions in Nampa could be expected to be depressed for some time to come.

Yet, the paper reminded Nampans that if anyone was at fault, it was those who had too much confidence in the development of Nampa at a time "when everything was at high tide." "We were all a little too optimistic perhaps," the paper conceded.

Although the vice president of the bank assured Nampans on the day of the closure that "the assets will cover all liabilities" and "the bank will pay out in full," by December of 1914 Eustace Smallwood, the receiver for the bank, had awarded dividends to depositors amounting to only thirty-five percent of their claims. While $87,036.65 was paid back to depositors, the total amount of claims filed against the bank amounted to $243,455.02. Nampans felt a financial pinch brought on by this crisis.

CITY POLITICS

In 1910 the Socialist Party became active in Nampa after Anna Maley, a party organizer who had a national reputation, came to speak in the town. The local Republican newspaper, the Nampa Leader-Herald, reported that she was well received when she lectured to large crowds at two separate gatherings, one an outdoor meeting on the Bank of Nampa corner and a second meeting in the evening at Conservatory Hall. The newspaper found Maley rather convincing, noting that:

> Those who attended her lecture last night, those who were already of that belief, went away much enthused, and those who attended merely as matter of curiosity, left the hall convinced that there is something to the socialist doctrines after all.

Following Maley's evening meeting a socialist local was organized in Nampa with a charter membership of fourteen men and

The Nampa City Hall, a cream-colored two-story brick building, was constructed on the corner of Twelfth Avenue and Second Street South in 1910. (CCHS)

two women. Frank Stewart headed the organization. A. B. Conley was corresponding secretary and Frank Page was financial secretary. The group obtained a room in the Brandt building for a Socialist Party headquarters.

In the next few weeks the Socialists regularly ran a column in the Leader-Herald explaining their views to the citizens of Nampa and asking people to approach the Socialist philosophy with an open mind. Their goal was pure and simple, according to the columnist, that being "to better conditions" by providing the working class a greater share of the wealth through public ownership of the means of production and distribution. A Nampan authored the columns but signed them "Local Socialist" instead of using his or her name.

By February of 1911 the Socialists of Nampa definitely had the attention of the town. When they invited the community to join them at a program and supper sponsored by the local party, over five hundred Nampans attended the social event. The paper reported that the group overflowed Prescott hall and many "could not find even standing room inside the doors." The program included orchestra music, a speech on the principles of socialism by a Boise organizer, "an entertaining reading," a vocal solo, and talks by local Socialist followers. Following the program, supper was served.

A little over a week later, Nampa Socialists participated in a day set aside nationally for a Socialist demonstration. This time the meeting was of a purely political nature, rather than being a social event, but attendance was still high. Held at the Orpheum Theater, the meeting drew a near capacity crowd.

By the end of February, the local party announced its plans to participate in Nampa's city election. Two years earlier voters had chosen between E. H. Dewey, who ran for mayor on the Citizens Party, and Eugene Emerson, who represented the Taxpayers Party. The two parties differed little in their platforms or policies, according to the newspaper, and thus "the campaign was necessarily along personal lines." Dewey was elected mayor by a majority of 313 votes out of 1198 votes cast.

During Dewey's tenure in office, opposition developed to his administration, the main point of contention being that city assessments which supported an improvement campaign were too high. The Socialists promised an alternative to the Dewey administration and rallied those who opposed the status quo.

Naming a complete ticket, the Nampa Socialists anticipated a lively campaign. Jesse Gardner, a photographer, headed their ticket, running for mayor against Dewey. Socialist candidates for councilmen included Mr. Baltazor, foreman at the brewery; Walter Jennings, of the Gowen blacksmith shop; Richard Edwards, proprietor of the Idaho rooming house; Frank Page, a shoe repairman; Roy Edwards, the city sidewalk inspector; and William Heszler, of the Robb clothing store. All of the candidates were active members of the Nampa Socialist local which by February of 1911 had 180 members.

The Socialist party made a particular effort to cater to the church crowd. Rumor had it that the "church people" had agreed to support the Socialist party in the upcoming election if "the right kind of candidates were selected." This was nothing more than rumor, reported the newspaper, but "some of the recognized leaders of the so-called 'church people'" attended the Socialist nominating meeting.

Edward H. Dewey, son of Colonel William Dewey, was mayor of Nampa from 1909 to 1913. (CCHS)

Mayors of Nampa

W. J. McClelland	1901 - 1903
Frank Sutherland	1903 - 1904
Henry A. Partridge	1904 - 1905
R. W. Purdum	1905 - 1907
Henry A. Partridge	1907 - 1909
Edward H. Dewey	1909 - 1913
Henry A. Partridge	1913 - 1915
Thomas Munhall	1915 - 1917
Robert Davis, Jr.	1917 - 1919
Howard H. Keim	1919 - 1921
J. Fremont Bow	1921 - 1923
Eugene Emerson	1923 - 1925
George Meffan	1925 - 1929
Eustace Smallwood	1929 - 1930
Windsor Lloyd	1930 - 1933
Evert W. Rising	1933 - 1935
George I. Van Name	1935 - 1937
R. Lewis Ord	1937 - 1939
Ben H. Waigand	1939 - 1943
Albert E. Lindsey	1943 - 1945
Sevren G. Honstead	1945 - 1947
Peter Johnson	1947 - 1951
Preston Capell	1951 - 1957
Thomas A. Leupp	1957 - 1961
Ernest Starr	1961 - 1981
Winston K. Goering	1982 -

J. Fremont Bow May 1921 - April 1923

Eustace Smallwood May 1929 - June 1930

George I. Van Name May 1935 - April 1937

R. Lewis Ord   May 1937 - April 1939

Sevren G. Honstead   May 1945 - June 1947

Thomas A. Leupp   May 1957 - April 1961

Peter Johnson   July 1947 - April 1951

(Photos courtesy Nampa City Hall)

Later known as the Parkhouse, E. H. Dewey built an elaborate residence in 1898 which overlooked Lake Ethel in Lakeview Park. (ISHS)

When the Citizens and the Taxpayers parties realized that the Socialist ticket might be a threat if the vote was divided in a three way race, they began discussing the possibility of a fusion ticket. Toward the end of March, the Taxpayers Party agreed not to field a slate of candidates for the upcoming election. That left the Socialists offering the only alternative to those who were disenchanted with the Dewey administration.

Both sides claimed victory before the election, although the Citizens Party seemed a little more sure of itself. The Socialists knew that if they carried the election, it would be a surprise for the town of Nampa, but, nevertheless, the Citizens Party admitted that "there was a feeling of uncertainty prevalent as to just what the strength of the opposition would prove to be." The Nampa Leader-Herald editorialized strongly in favor of the Citizens Party candidates.

When the votes were cast, the Dewey administration remained in office and the Citizens Party maintained control of the city government. Out of 1262 votes cast, Dewey garnered 740 votes while Gardner received 501 votes for mayor. Dewey won by a majority of 239 votes.

Even though they were defeated at the polls, the Socialists remained active in Nampa. They continued to hold street meetings in which they attempted to educate the public as to their philosophy. At one such gathering in September of 1911, a clash developed between the local Socialists and the police department when Chief of Police Maloney refused to allow them to sell books without a license. The Socialist organizers "made some very uncomplimentary remarks about the police and city regulations in general" but by the next Saturday when they met again, the Socialists had obtained permission from city officials to sell their books.

In 1913 when it came time once more for city elections, the Socialists were again ready to participate. Dewey chose not to run for a third term and so the Citizens Party had to seek a new face to represent its interests. It nominated H. A. Partridge to run for

Lake Ethel, a man-made irrigation reservoir, filled the bowl area of Lakeview Park until it was drained in the mid-1920s. (ISHS)

mayor but made it clear that they were content with the status quo by adopting a resolution endorsing the Dewey administration of the past two years.

The Socialists nominated Royal W. Edwards, a stockman, to run for mayor along with a full slate of candidates for clerk and police judge, treasurer and councilmen. There were no other parties competing in the election.

The election failed to generate the interest drawn by the 1911 contest. Overall the Socialists polled fewer votes than two years earlier. However, for the only time in the city's history they put a Socialist candidate into office. In the Third Ward, L.C. McCarty, who ran on the Socialist ticket, gained fifty-nine per cent of the vote to defeat G. H. Moore, the Citizens nominee.

Now the Socialists had a voice on the city council, the official organ of the town. However, that did not mean that their wishes were always granted. In February of 1914 the Socialists presented to the council a petition containing about 400 names asking that the assembly room in the city hall be made available for public meetings. The council denied the request with Councilman McCarty

Skating on Lake Ethel was a popular winter pastime in the early part of the century. (ISHS)

the only one voting in favor of the petition. Following the denial of the Socialists' request, the city council adopted a resolution closing the city hall to all organizational meetings except for the Chamber of Commerce, the Grand Army of the Republic and the Women's Relief Corps.

When city election time rolled around again in the spring of 1915, the Leader-Herald noted a "remarkable lack of interest" in the upcoming contest. Mayor Partridge declined to run for reelection, leaving the race open. Initially, the Socialist Party voted not to field a slate of candidates, but after the Citizens Party selected its nominees, the Socialists reconsidered.

A week before the election, a third party, calling itself the Independents, entered the race. They endorsed the work of Mayor Partridge and three incumbent councilmen, including L. C. McCarty, the 1913 Socialist victor. McCarty, however, chose to run for reelection on the Independent ticket. Although the Socialists warned that any member of their party who supported a candidate on any other ticket would be expelled, they also made a public statement declaring that they had no opposition to any of the Citizens or Independent Party candidates.

In the final few days before the election, the campaign heated up. The Citizens Party ran a rather lengthy article in the newspaper distinguishing itself from the Independents which they referred to as "the grouch ticket." It also criticized all sixteen nominees on the Independent ticket for failing to belong to the Nampa Chamber of Commerce.

When the votes were counted, T. E. Munhall, candidate of the Independent Party, was elected mayor with fifty-eight per cent of the vote cast in the three way race. He soundly defeated E. Smallwood, the Citizens Party candidate, and H. J. Stuart, the Socialist nominee, and took into office with him seven other Independent Party candidates. Only two Citizens Party candidates remained in office, and one of these was Miss Gertrude Miller who had no opposition in her reelection bid as city treasurer.

The 1915 city election signified two things. The strength of the Citizens Party, which had consistently rallied a majority of the

Indian Creek flooded in 1916, covering the town with water. This photo was taken from a telephone pole on the corner of Fifteenth Avenue and Second Street North. (ISHS)

votes in the past several elections, was broken. The coalition of interests which formed the Independent Party remained a viable force in city politics for the next several years. Furthermore, the Socialists, who had been a relatively strong second party in Nampa city elections, had passed their peak. They never again witnessed the support that they possessed in the early years of the 1910 decade.

TRANSPORTATION

When Nampa was founded, the railroad provided the connecting link between the community and the outside world. Within the town of Nampa and the surrounding countryside, the horse and buggy was the main mode of travel as late as 1914. However, mass transit came to the area in 1909 with the development of the electric streetcar system, commonly called the Interurban.

Boise had electric trolleys as early as 1891, yet it was 1906 before interest developed in putting trolley lines into Nampa, and then, several individuals had the same idea. In March of 1906, the Nampa City Council gave permission to E. H. Dewey to operate an electric railway over city streets. Dewey's transportation system was to be completed and in operation within eighteen months.

The Interurban Railroad, shown on First Street South, came to Nampa in 1909 and was the main mode of transportation in the valley until widespread use of automobiles and commercial trucks put the Interurban out of business in May of 1928. (CCHS)

In late summer of the same year, three separate enterprises announced plans to connect Nampa to the rest of the valley through an electric streetcar system. On August 20, Robert Noble, Dr. H. P. Ustick and W. N. Donaldson requested a franchise from the city for the Boise Valley Electric Railroad. On August 23, Walter E. Pierce and his associates announced plans for the Boise & Interurban Railway Company to expand their operation to Nampa. The city council granted their request for a franchise in September. Toward the end of the month of August, a third company headed by Sherman Coffin began securing right-of-ways for a line between Caldwell and Nampa, going through the Deer Flat area.

It was the line proposed by Robert Noble which finally entered Nampa, but not without years of delay. The project got off to a

These men are working on the power lines which provided the electricity to run the Interurban Railway trolleys. (ISHS)

promising start. On October 23, 1906, Noble and Dr. Ustick brought a large number of men to town to begin construction and drive the first spike of the Boise Valley Electric Railway in Nampa. The town was pleased that they had kept their promise to begin work early.

But by July of 1907, the city council felt it necessary to contact Noble's company regarding the slowness of the project. Noble answered that his company was involved in constructing a line from Caldwell to the Deer Flat recreation area, and thus delayed in getting into Nampa. Also, it was experiencing trouble in securing ties.

In October, the city council extended Noble's franchise for sixty days but set November 20, 1907 as a deadline for construction of tracks in the city. On that day, the company broke ground in Nampa and assured the public that it had not given up the venture. But the work stopped as quickly as it had begun. By February of 1908, Nampans were becoming skeptical because of the delays and by

August were demanding action or the cancellation of the franchise. By October, the company announced that it was within three miles of Nampa and was delayed by the failure of the city council to decide what type of bridge should go over Indian Creek. The city and the railroad company disputed who was to pay what share for the cost of the bridge, but even after this was settled, two more months passed without any action.

In April of 1909, the work that had previously been completed was found to be insufficient. Heavier rails had to be laid on streets that were to be paved. During the summer months, Noble assured the town that work was progressing rapidly, but the Boise Valley Electric Railroad did not begin service to Nampa until October 12, 1909.

The initial four hour trip between Boise and Nampa included an inspection of the trolley and the rails and a side trip to Meridian. The return to Boise was made in one hour and ten minutes. Passenger and freight service began operation immediately, even though the crossing over the Oregon Short Line was not completed into Nampa until December.

But still, no interurban service connected Nampa and Caldwell. In the summer of 1911, a group of concerned citizens held a meeting at the Midway School to promote the completion of this phase of the project. This group obtained right-of-way contracts for the proposed line.

In October of 1911 when the Idaho-Oregon Light and Power Company bought out Robert Noble's Boise Valley Electric Railroad, the new owners expressed interest in developing the Nampa-Caldwell line. Also, about that same time, the Boise & Interurban, which provided service in Boise, merged with the company just sold by Noble.

The new management planned improvements on the merged lines, including heavier rails, new Nampa and Caldwell stations, new cars and the completion of the line between Nampa and

The Boise Valley Electric Railroad began service to Nampa from Boise via Meridian on October 12, 1909. (ISHS)

Caldwell. The company kept its promises and the building of the Nampa-Caldwell line went smoothly. The first train took twenty minutes to make the trip between the two cities in May of 1912.

Not only was the electric railroad line used for business purposes, in particular the transportation of produce for the fruit growers, dairymen and farmers, but it also became a main source of entertainment. "Loop the Loop" excursions were a popular Sunday pastime. For a dollar, a person could tour between Caldwell and Boise with one stopover allowed at any point in addition to stops in Boise or Caldwell. Boise invited riders to visit the new Natatorium and Caldwell advertised a connecting line to the Lake Lowell recreation area where boating and fishing were available.

Ben Anketell recalled those days:

> For a number of years, why it was the thing on Sunday you could go around the loop for a dollar. And we used to board the streetcar on Sunday, and had nothing else to do, and go down through Caldwell and Boise and back to Nampa.

At first, the electric street cars ran at a maximum speed of twelve miles an hour, but, as the line became more efficient, the speed increased. In September of 1913, a Nampa city councilman expressed concern about the safety of the trolley line because of its speed. The city council threatened to pass an ordinance regulating the enterprise unless the cars slowed down. Coming in from Caldwell along Third Street South, the council estimated that the trolley cars often travelled at up to thirty-five to forty miles an hour.

As automobiles and commercial trucks became more widely used, the electric streetcar line began to experience increasingly serious financial difficulties. In 1915, bondholders forced the sale of the properties because of low returns on their investments. The Boise Valley Traction Company, with E. H. Dewey serving as

Shown here is the interior of one of the cars of the Interurban Railway. (ISHS)

president, took over management of the lines after a receiver's sale in the summer of 1915. Some business gains were made during the war years, but by 1924 the enterprise was in financial distress again.

Foreclosure proceedings were begun in 1925, but dragged on until Judge F. S. Dietrich set a foreclosure sale for May 17, 1928. On the day of the sale, the Boise Valley Traction Company, recognizing its inability to compete with automobiles and trucks, asked the Idaho Public Utilities Commission for permission to abandon service.

At the foreclosure sale, all hope of reviving the line was relinquished. The enterprise which had cost more than two million dollars to develop was sold for under ten cents on the dollar. Few spectators mourned the passing of an era when the last car left Boise at 6 p.m. and Caldwell at 6:30 p.m. In 1930 W. C. Dewey's Idaho Contracting Company covered the old trolley tracks in the city of Nampa and removed the remnants of a day gone by on the unpaved highways in the rural areas.

By now, the automobile had come of age. But, auto transportation was not always to be taken for granted. Prior to 1920, families used the automobile primarily as a pleasure vehicle, and then, it was not always easy going due to the conditions of the roads. Dr. Bob Mangum came to Nampa in 1918 when he was four years old. His earliest recollection of Nampa is of the streets "which were muddy and rutty and very difficult to get through. The cars would struggle and get stuck in the middle of the streets."

Sometimes horses were less trouble than autos. Ben Waigand remembers:

> A good team of horses would do the twenty miles to Boise in about two hours. The horses were left in the livery stables for feed and water and rest and returned the same day to Nampa on the all dirt highways, which was about as good time as some of the early cars would make it.

> When you entered Boise, it used to be a real

THE RAILROAD

For years, the railroad was the hub of Nampa. Much of the town's activities centered on the comings and the goings at the local depot. In addition, the railroad has been one of the major employers in the town, providing work for numerous Nampans. Called the Junction City, Nampa was a connecting point for several trains early in the Twentieth century. Passengers and businesses alike depended upon the railroad to join Nampa with the outlying world.

This Nampa train depot was used prior to 1903. It was moved to the town from King Hill on flat cars and set up in October of 1887. The cart in front is loaded with gold and silver bullion ready to be shipped from the Trade Dollar Mine in Silver City. (CCHS)

Nampa's second train depot was built in 1903. This picture shows Front Street, looking north with the brewery and Tuttle Mercantile visible in the background. (ISHS)

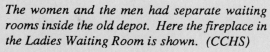

The women and the men had separate waiting rooms inside the old depot. Here the fireplace in the Ladies Waiting Room is shown. (CCHS)

The ticket counter of the depot displays ornate wood carvings. (ISHS)

Ben Doles and R.C. Blakeslee are shown in the office of the train depot. (CCHS)

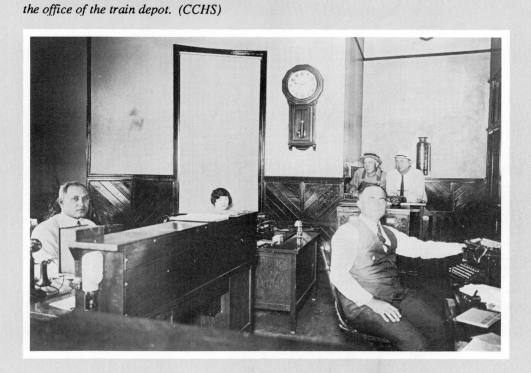

Oregon Short Line Engine number 403 is shown here in approximately 1918. The Dewey Palace is visible in the background. (ISHS)

A roundhouse, built by the railroad in Nampa, opened in March of 1917. Initially, it employed a crew of forty mechanics who serviced thirty-eight engines headquartered in Nampa's railroad yards. (ISHS)

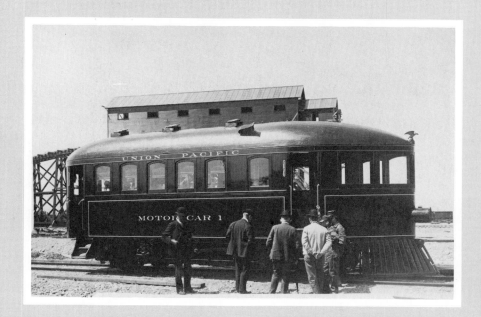

A Union Pacific motor car is shown in front of the coal chute in Nampa's railroad yard. (ISHS)

A new $160,000 Union Pacific depot opened in Nampa in 1925. This depot served the town until Union Pacific discontinued passenger service in 1974. (ISHS)

Remembering back, John Brandt described coming to town on a Saturday night as a youngster. Automobiles played a part in the scene:

That was a big night! Saturday afternoon, in fact, was a big day for all the farmers. The farmers came to town. The stores were all open. They hitched their horses to the rack and spent the whole afternoon visiting. Then the people who were occupied, wage earners or farm hands and the young people, came out Saturday night to shop and visit.

At that time there were no regulations against it, but one of the things we kids got a kick out of was opening the "cut-out." We had what was called a "cut-out" in the exhaust. It gave us great pleasure driving back and forth on Main Street opening that "cut-out" to make all the noise we could. We had a little lighted radiator cap that rotated. We would drive back and forth opening that "cut-out" to attract attention then shut it off so they would see our radiator cap. Boy, these crazy things I haven't thought about for years!

steep hill there and coming back out of Boise the hill was so steep that the early cars had trouble getting up there. You had to go in low gear to get up that hill to get out of Boise.

When cars would make the trip, it was usually necessary to repair several flat tires on a round trip to Boise and back to Nampa. You had to take the tire off the rim to fix the tire, or to fix the innertube or patch the innertube, put it back together again and pump it up. The horses, they just kept on going.

But, nonetheless, Nampans had "automobile fever." By October of 1909, the Leader-Herald reported that there were over twenty cars in town, up from five cars owned by Nampans a year earlier. The Buick was the most popular make of car in Nampa, although Fords ranked next in number.

The newspaper credited Charlie Robbins with owning the "pioneer machine" in town. Robbins used his Wayne two-cylinder car extensively, according to the paper, and was "one of the few who have discovered the value and convenience of the automobile to the practical business man." Even Robbins' twelve-year-old son, Harvey, was often seen driving the car around town and was thought to be "as efficient a chaufeur as his distinguished father."

In March of 1908, Henry E. Bradley and Stewart Mateer, owners of the Dewey Livery Barn, bought a red two-cylinder Reo Tonneau which would hold five people. With this car, Nampa's first auto taxi service was initiated. For twenty-five cents, Bradley or Mateer would take passengers anywhere in the city or, for a reasonable fee, they would even drive out of town. Ben Waigand recalled:

Henry Bradley had the first Nampa taxi and for a fee would go to Givens Hot Springs on the Snake River or to Boise. It was common on these long trips to repair several flats. The roads were dirt, full of chuck holes, and often after a rain one would get stuck and found it necessary to fill brush under the rear wheels or to get a horse to pull the car to better ground.

By 1909, Bradley and Mateer's taxi service was popular

Charlie Robbins owned the first car in Nampa, shown here with the Robbins' family. Even Robbins' twelve-year-old son, Harvey, was often seen driving the car around town. (Courtesy, Eric Robbins)

enough that they added a four-passenger Buick No. 10. "These cars are kept busy practically all the time," the paper reported.

Initially, the towns took responsibility for licensing automobiles rather than the state. Licensing began as early as 1905 in Idaho, but Nampa waited until the summer of 1910 to require all car owners to register and license their vehicles. For an annual fee of $2.50, the car owner received a red metal tag bearing the name of the town, Nampa, and a number. The licenses were about fourteen inches long and four and a half inches wide and the city provided a strap which was to be used to fasten the "tag" to the rear of the car. Those who failed to license their cars were subject to a $100 fine.

By August, twenty-three cars had been registered with the city and the newspaper reported that there were at least seven more car owners who had yet to take out licenses. Some questioned the necessity for licensing cars, but the city clerk contended, "The addition of one of these tags to high-geared, wide-gauge automobiles is supposed to keep the car from exceeding the eight-mile speed limit of the city." However, "his guarantee has already been shown to be worthless," reported the Leader-Herald, adding, "The tag might aid in identifying remains in case of accident."

Nampans traded cars often in the early years of automobile ownership. In the spring of 1911, for example, W. C. Dewey anticipated the arrival of his new Cadillac car which was to take the place of last year's "E. M. F." Dr. Murray was buying a new car "for use in aiding the stork bird," replacing his Ford run-about. Dr. Joyner reported that he couldn't afford "to keep up to style by getting a new car this spring," but he proposed "to deceive the

Nampans began buying automobiles during the first decade after the turn of the century. By October of 1909, the local newspaper reported that there were over twenty cars in town and that Nampans had "automobile fever." (ISHS)

The Showalter Chevrolet showroom displays the latest in new cars. (CCHS)

public by having his white Buick of last year given a coat of black paint with red trimmings."

The Leader-Herald reported that there were numerous prospective car owners in Nampa in March of 1911. Many were giving in to "the fever." One car dealership had the "right system" for promoting sales, according to the newspaper. The dealer gave "a trial ride" during which the prospective buyer was "allowed to take the wheel, to run the car himself." This assured the sale. "Let a man once get hold of the wheel and he is lost," noted the paper.

Sales improved if the car dealer emphasized the value of the automobile for business, even though the cars were used mainly for pleasure. The newspaper commented:

The Edmark Automobile Company was located on the north corner of Second Street and Thirteen Avenue South in the mid-1920s. A 1925 Dodge is parked in front of the showroom. (CCHS)

The Showalter Chevrolet Garage located on Third Street South serviced various makes of cars including this 1925 Model T Ford. (CCHS)

In many cases all that is necessary to make a sale is to supply the prospect with the excuse that he is purchasing the machine for business purposes, that it will pay him in time saved for its cost and up-keep. There are few willing to acknowledge that they are investing a thousand or more for pleasure purposes only.

With the cars, came the hazards. In March of 1911, the Leader-Herald reported, "With the opening of the automobile season, the public is again menaced by the reckless driving of automobiles on the streets of the city." A city ordinance set the speed limit for the town at eight miles per hour, but this was often overlooked, according to the paper, by drivers who "dash recklessly down the street at a speed varying from fifteen to twenty-five miles an hour." Because the police department overlooked such offenses, "the lives of people on the streets [are] endangered several times every hour of the day."

In July the city council tried to deal with automobile safety by passing a new city ordinance which raised the speed limit to twelve miles an hour, directed drivers to use the right side of the street "as

As the use of automobiles increased, car accidents became a constant menace to society. (ISHS)

much as possible," and warned automobilists to exercise care "where frightened horses are encountered." Careless driving was punishable by a $100 fine.

But the inevitable could not be avoided. With the advent of automobiles came automobile accidents. Some happened because of the novelty of the "machines." For example, in September of 1913, T. W. Brown, a rancher in the Nampa area, was killed when his horses which were pulling a mowing machine became frightened at a passing motorcycle. "They dashed down the road and ran straightway into a barb wire fence along the highway, throwing the driver from the seat of the machine headlong into the fence," reported the newspaper. Dr. Murray and Dr. Ross performed surgery, but Brown died about a day after the accident.

Some accidents occurred because the drivers were speeding. Such was the case with Arthur L. Hulbert who was killed in June of 1914 when "the Ford machine which he was driving turned turtle at the sharp turn after crossing the tracks of the Interurban line pinning him and his four companions beneath the car" at the corner of Eighth Street and Sugar Avenue. Hulbert's companions escaped with only minor injuries, but the car was completely wrecked. "The body was broken and twisted, fenders crushed, back wheel broken out, tire stripped from one of the front wheels, steering gear bent, fenders crushed and lamps broken."

Only a few days later, another fatal accident occurred near Midway when L. A. Goldsmith, a contractor from Caldwell, was "attempting to make his little machine keep pace with a big gray car which was speeding in the direction of Nampa." Goldsmith lost control of his "little Ford" and it "turned over twice within a distance of about 35 feet." He was killed instantly from a broken neck but two companions received only scratches.

As late as 1939, Nampa's traffic control was still quite unsophisticated. Ben Waigand was elected mayor of Nampa that year. Looking back, he noted:

> Traffic control in Nampa was nil. There
> wasn't any. The car that sounded his horn

first at the intersection usually got the right of way. The fender business flourished here.

We bought eight Westinghouse street corner traffic lights which were installed at the busiest town intersections. They did a great job but it is hard to change anything without a lot of people being against traffic light, or anything I should have said.

They didn't like the idea of being stopped by the traffic light if they hit the intersection when traffic was going at right angles to them. Others thought it was a waste of taxpayer's money and too advanced for Nampa traffic. Imagine the traffic jams Nampa would have today without traffic lights and the horn noise from the cars trying to beat the other cars to the corner. I don't think Nampa could afford enough traffic officers to answer all the accidents which would undoubtedly happen without the traffic lights.

Ben H. Waigand was mayor of Nampa in 1939 when traffic lights were first installed at some Nampa intersections. (Courtesy, Nampa City Hall)

THE HARVEST FESTIVAL

Anxious to display the produce of the region, Nampa's farmers joined together with the town's businessmen in August of 1911, organizing the first Nampa Harvest Festival, or "The Fair Without a Fence". This event became a popular annual affair, complete with displays of grains, fruits, and vegetables; refreshment stands; a barbecue; and special entertainment including foot races, band concerts, dances, and theater programs. In subsequent years a horse show, carnival amusements, a street dance, a parade, and special contests were added to the program.

People crowd the streets, enjoying the displays and exhibits of the Nampa Harvest Festival. (CCHS)

At the 1919 Harvest Festival, Fred Mock appeared as "Chief Nampah". His impersonation was so convincing that he set a legend in motion that Nampa was named after an Indian warchief.

The final Harvest Festival was held in September of 1937. The next year the rodeo portion of the Harvest Festival broke away from the rest of the fair and continued the tradition of community entertainment, becoming known as the Snake River Stampede. A "Home Products Show" was held in the autumn, a couple of months after the rodeo, but the Harvest Festival, as such, was never revived.

Refreshment stands join displays in attracting the people of Nampa to the Harvest Festival. Les King, Sam Hughart, B. L. Johnsohn, and E. R. Braie are shown here among others on the Dewey Palace lawn. (CCHS)

Mrs. Robert C. Blakeslee rides as queen of the Harvest Festival in 1914. Mayor Henry A. Partridge, among others, joins her. (CCHS)

Keim's Meat Market participated in a Harvest Festival Parade in 1918 with this Cold Storage Market delivery wagon. William Keim is the driver. (CCHS)

These farmers proudly display their produce in a float prepared for a Harvest Festival parade. (Courtesy, Mary Henshall)

The best of the area's produce is exhibited in displays prepared by the area's farmers. (Courtesy, Jerry Cornilles)

IV
Institutional Development:
1910 - 1920

In the first couple of decades of its existence, the town of Nampa firmly established itself as a stable community. As it approached the second decade of the twentieth century, Nampa turned its attention to developing institutions which would refine and educate its people and provide for their physical and moral welfare. In addition, the town convinced the state to establish a major state institution, the Idaho State Sanitarium, near the city limits.

NORTHWEST NAZARENE COLLEGE

Northwest Nazarene College was started by a layman in the Church of the Nazarene who never preached a sermon and did not have a college education himself. Eugene Emerson, born 1866 in Ohio, came to Idaho by covered wagon with his family when he was sixteen years old. The family settled in American Ridge in Latah County, Idaho. After Eugene's father, James Emerson, died in 1900, Mrs. Emerson sold their property and moved to Marsing, Idaho, where she took out a homestead.

After returning to Kansas and marrying his boyhood sweetheart, Indiana Bogue, Eugene decided to settle in Nampa after the turn of the century. Here Emerson bought and sold livestock until in 1904 he started a lumber business, which he later sold to Windsor Lloyd.

In the summer of 1913 Eugene Emerson went to Boise to attend the first general meeting of the recently organized Oregon-Idaho District of the Nazarene Church. At this assembly, the education committee stressed the secular nature of public education, commenting that "God's work is woefully neglected in the public schools and higher institutions of our district." They recommended that "all who know the value of souls" should either "educate their children at home by private instructors, or as soon as practicable, arrange for private church schools."

Eugene Emerson founded Northwest Nazarene College in 1913. (Courtesy, N.N.C.)

Facing Page: In July of 1915, Rev. Lewis Hadley and Harry Hays broke ground for Northwest Nazarene College's first building. (Courtesy, N.N.C.)

The District was so slow in reaching a decision about the location of the school, debating between Spokane, Washington or Nampa, that Emerson went ahead on his own. He and M. E. Ferdinand, the first pastor of the Nazarene Church in Nampa, rented a small Mennonite church building on the corner of Eighth Street and Thirteenth Avenue South and convinced Carlton and Emma French of Troy, Idaho, to move to Nampa to be principal and teacher. Miss Gladys Bellamy, Mrs. French's sister, came with them to teach part time.

Mrs. French later reminisced:

> Mr. French and I prayed over these letters and accepted the offer. We sold all of our belongings and like Abraham of old went out not knowing where we were going. I wondered if I would ever see my mother, father, brother, and sisters again, who lived near us. Mr. French said goodbye to his mother for the last time.

> We were met at the depot in Nampa by Eugene Emerson. We had neither one ever been in an automobile and had vowed to each other that we never would. But when Mr. Emerson put our luggage in his car, we looked at each other, and crawled in. We felt strange, but it was only one of the things we did that we never thought we would do.

In September of 1913 the school opened with thirteen elementary school students. In an all day meeting attended by members and pastors of the Caldwell, Nampa and Boise Nazarene Churches, suspicion of public education was again voiced. "We look forward to a great institution in which the youth of the Church may be protected from the erroneous teaching frequently met in the public school system," the school organizers noted. The institution,

The first boys' dorm, used in 1913, was called "the den" or "the shack." (Courtesy, N.N.C.)

however, planned its curriculum in accordance with the requirements of the state manual for elementary work, adding Bible classes to the regular course work.

The school felt a great deal of stress during its opening semester. The French family was to be paid one hundred dollars a month plus moving expenses, but from the beginning financing was difficult. Mrs. French recalled:

> We worked very hard in the school, taught in the morning and made calls in the afternoon, and attended a mission at night, which M. E. Ferdinand had charge of. The finances did not come in as they had planned. We never received any money, but our house was furnished and our grocery bill was finally paid.

When Reverend Ferdinand, president of the school, decided that financial conditions dictated that the school be made independent of the Nazarene Church, he called the Frenchs to his home to discuss his decision. They were unwilling to see the infant institution sever its ties to the Nazarene Church and, consequently, Ferdinand requested their resignation. In the middle of winter,

These early Nazarene academy students posed for this picture in 1914. Lowell H. Coate and Charles V. Marshall were the teachers. (Courtesy, N.N.C.)

N.N.C.'s new administration building was not ready when it came time to start classes in the fall of 1915 and so the students met in the chapel built by Eugene Emerson for church services on Fifteenth Avenue and Sixth Street South. Standing on the steps of the building are Earl, Calvin and Martha Emerson. (Courtesy, N.N.C.)

without employment or money, the Frenchs resigned.

After operating during its second year with an independent status, the school received the support of the District Assembly of the Church of the Nazarene in the spring of 1915. The group elected trustees and raised approximately $6000 for the construction of a suitable building for the institution. In July of the same year, the school's promoters broke ground for a building in the midst of sagebrush on a tract of land located some distance south of any other dwellings in the town of Nampa, "blocks and blocks from any city street."

The new administration building was not ready when it came time to start classes in the fall and so the students met in the Chapel built by Emerson for church services on Fifteenth Avenue and Sixth Street South. The conditions here were less than ideal; "there was ample noise, classes got in each other's way, and often enough the stove smoked!"

But in November, students and faculty made a long march to the new campus and began occupancy of the first structure built just for the school. When the students reached the new campus, they entered the administration building via stout planks, for the steps had yet to be built.

The first building constructed on the Northwest Nazarene College campus is still the main structure of the present administration building. Changes were made in the original building in 1931. (Courtesy, N.N.C.)

Going to and from the school was not an easy task. "There was no sidewalk out from town and Holly Street was not paved. In dry weather the road was covered with several inches of fine powdery dust, and in wet weather it was sticky with mud." Immediately following the move the road became nearly impassable because of the rain, but the boys and men carried the girls and young ladies "over the small lakes and puddles, which were up to fifty or more feet across."

By November 24, 1915 when the Nazarenes dedicated the new building, school enrollment had reached 115. The school offered college work for the first time during this year with five students enrolled in the two-year college curriculum. The 1916-1917 school catalog was the first to mention the name Northwest Nazarene College.

By commencement in June of 1917, "students were graduated from all four departments of the institution --- fourteen from the Elementary School, seven from the Academy, two from the Bible

These students were part of the student body of the school in 1915 when enrollment reached 115. (Courtesy, N.N.C.)

Dr. H. Orton Wiley was the first president of N.N.C. (Courtesy, N.N.C.)

Right: Professor C. V. Marshall poses with the first high school class on the steps of the administration building in 1915. The main door of the building had not yet been hung. (Courtesy, N.N.C.)

Dr. Olive Winchester was vice-president and dean of N.N.C. from 1923 to 1935. (Courtesy, N.N.C.)

course, and four from the College of Liberal Arts." Furthermore, the school had brought a number of families to Nampa. The Nampa Leader-Herald, on November 30, 1917, reported that the institution was responsible for seventy-one families moving to Nampa. Thirty-eight of these had purchased property and another thirty-three families were renting. The newspaper estimated that these Nazarene families would expend a total of $70,000 a year in Nampa. In addition, the article valued the college property at $52,931.

In the spring of 1917, Northwest Nazarene College greeted its first president, Dr. H. Orton Wiley. Dr. Wiley found that the physical plant of the school consisted of an administration building and two unfinished dormitories located on "a campus of eight city blocks of desert land from which the sagebrush had been removed in favor of the rather more prolific crop of tumbleweeds." There was very little academic equipment --- "no organized library, and very little scientific apparatus."

Yet, for a small school, the faculty was surprisingly strong in academic training. In 1917 the teaching faculty included three who held master's degrees --- Dr. Wiley, Professor Charles V. Marshall, M.S. from Penn College, and Professor Mary I. Forsythe. College coursework was offered in English, history, mathematics, science, philosophy, theology and religion, Spanish, art and applied music.

In the fall of 1917, Olive M. Winchester joined the faculty. Her academic background was impressive. She graduated from Radcliffe College, of Harvard University, received the B.D. degree from Glasgow University, "the first woman to be granted that degree in that institution," and completed a master's degree in theology at the Pacific School of Religion. As a professor she taught Bible courses and sociology. Then she became vice-president and dean of the college, positions which she held until she resigned in 1935.

In the fall of 1918, Dr. T.E. Mangum came to Nampa, joining with the school to open a nurses' department with the purpose of giving prospective missionaries medical training. Eventually a separate board of trustees was placed over this department and this

SAMARITAN HOSPITAL

In 1921, the Nazarene Missionary Sanitarium and Institute moved into the former residence of Dr. and Mrs. T.E. Mangum, utilizing the facility not only to train nurses but also as a hospital. (Courtesy, N.N.C.)

Construction work began on Samaritan Hospital in 1926, but slowed during the Depression years. The hospital presented its new facilities to the community at an open house in May of 1934. In 1936, the north wing was added, providing an obstetrics and maternity ward. (Courtesy, N.N.C.)

Samaritan continued to offer nurses' training in conjunction with N.N.C. during the 1930s. (Courtesy, N.N.C.)

This operating room scene at Samaritan was typical of the age in 1936. (Courtesy, N.N.C.)

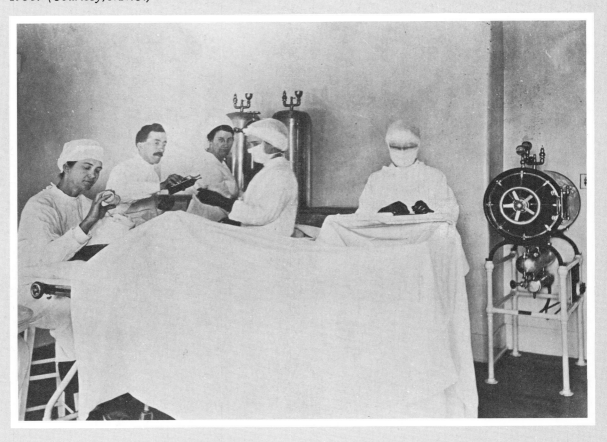

Twelfth Avenue, between Front Street and First Street, was the heart of Nampa's business district during the early days of the town. Recently renovated, the area contains enterprises which combine new form with the old character of the region. (Photo left, courtesy Winston K Goering; photo below by Robert E. Lee.)

In 1908, when J. J. HasBrouck constructed his residence, it was located some distance from the town. In the 1980's developers renovated the structure keeping it true to its original character. It now houses a restaurant, antique shop and real estate office. (Photo by Jim Thomas)

Wall street borders the east side of the new Longbranch development in downtown Nampa. This area was the headquarters of the Chinese population in town just after the turn of the century. (Photo by Jim Thomas)

Nampa's new city hall was constructed in 1982. The 1.2 million dollar structure houses the city administration in an efficient and attractive setting. (Photo by Jim Thomas)

When the old Oregon Short Line depot, built in 1903, was threatened with demolition in 1972, concerned citizens organized the Canyon County Historical Society and worked to save the structure. After Union Pacific donated the building to the historical society, volunteer labor painstakingly restored the depot to its original character. (Photo right, courtesy ISHS; photo below by Robert E. Lee)

Nampa was established because of its location on the Oregon Short Line railroad. The trains continue to provide a major transportation system for area businesses and industries. (Photo by Bill Grange, courtesy Nampa Chamber of Commerce)

In the early days, fishing on the Snake River close to Nampa was thought to be a "profitable pastime" as shown in this historic color postcard. (Courtesy, CCHS)

The central unit of Kenwood School was built in 1901 when the growth of Nampa's school population dictated the need for additional classroom space. By 1909, two additions had been added to the school. (Courtesy, CCHS)

This structure, built in 1907, replaced Nampa's first Lakeview school which was erected in 1892. At the time of its opening, the Nampa Leader-Herald boasted that the new Lakeview School was "the finest school building in Idaho". (Courtesy, CCHS)

A quarter-million-dollar structure, the Dewey Palace, built in 1902, rose "like a castle in a barren waste." Transcontinental train travelers regarded Nampa's hotel as the plushest hotel between Omaha, Nebraska, and Portland, Oregon. (Courtesy, CCHS)

Lake Ethel, Nampa, Idaho. No. 5

Lake Ethel, an irrigation reservoir formed when Mason Creek was dammed, enjoyed a high reputation as a recreation spot in the early days of Nampa's history. It was a popular boating spot in the summer and a favorite skating pond in the winter. (Courtesy, CCHS)

A typical Residence, Nampa, Idaho. No. 6

The E. H. Dewey residence, built in 1899, was called a typical Nampa residence in this early postcard. However, it was far from it. Most Nampa homes were of a more modest means. (Courtesy, CCHS)

Ample irrigation water combines with fertile soil and a favorable climate to make good agricultural production possible in the Nampa area. (Photo by Jim Thomas)

Demonstrating the diversity of crops grown in the Nampa area, this onion field presents a pleasing scene. (Photo by Jim Thomas)

Crops grown in the Nampa area include everything from famous Idaho potatoes to sugar beets, corn, fruit and grain. (Photo by Jim Thomas)

Sailing is a popular pastime on Lake Lowell, south of Nampa. (Photo by Jim Thomas)

Lakeview Park provides the town with a picturesque and spacious area for recreation-seekers. Nampans enjoy a quiet stroll or a lively game of softball in the park. (Photo by Bill Grange, courtesy Nampa Chamber of Commerce)

Winter leaves its markings along this irrigation creek which, during the summer, carries the lifeblood of the fields nearby. (Photo by Jim Thomas)

Nampans enjoy a variety of weather conditions and a definite delineation of the four seasons of the year. Rain can occur anytime, however. (Photo by Jim Thomas)

The Snake River Stampede began as a rodeo in conjunction with the Nampa Harvest Festival. When the Harvest Festival was discontinued in 1937, the Stampede continued, gaining a reputation as a major event in the world of rodeo. (Photo by Jim Thomas)

The Stampede Stagecoach promotes Nampa's summertime rodeo throughout the valley. It can be seen nightly at the Stampede circling the arena. (Photo by Jim Thomas)

The land surrounding Nampa has gone from sagebrush-covered desert to fertile farm lands because of irrigation. (Photos by Jim Thomas)

Spray planes often break the silence of the evening, furnishing the farmers with a necessary service. (Photos by Jim Thomas)

The Deer Flat Reservoir, named Lake Lowell in February of 1948, was built to provide irrigation for the area. Protected by a federal game reserve, Canadian geese are often seen in the area in the spring and fall. (Photo by Jim Thomas)

effort evolved into the establishment of Samaritan Hospital.

After making the move to the new campus, the school grew rapidly. In the school year 1915-16, the enrollment was 133, yet three years later that figure had grown to 342. When Dr. Wiley came in 1917, he clearly saw that additional facilities were needed.

However, the greatest challenge facing Dr.Wiley as N.N.C.'s new president was the problem of financial support. Dr. Wiley found the raising of money for the college to be "unbelievably hard" in those days. Remembering one particular fund-raising trip, Dr. Wiley recalled:

> Mr. Herrell and I decided to make a trip through the Northwest to see if we could raise some money. Before we left I laid the matter before the students, telling them that we had to have $8,000 by some means. A little fellow on the front seat piped up, 'I have faith for ten thousand dollars.' I looked at him and thought, 'You poor ignoramus, you have no idea how much ten thousand dollars amounts to when you have to raise it by solicitation.' We visited Walla Walla and received enough help from there to go to the next place, and in this manner made that preliminary trip. When we returned, we had ten thousand dollars in cash and subscriptions.

Dr. Thomas E. Mangum opened a nurses' department at N.N.C. in the fall of 1918 with the purpose of giving medical training to prospective missionaries. This effort evolved into the establishment of Samaritan Hospital. (Courtesy, Frances Mangum)

In February of 1919 a Victory Campaign was launched with the chief objective being to raise money for the building fund. An all day service opened this campaign and at the close of the day $28,000 had been pledged. The campaign committee held meetings through the Northwest during the summer months and all in all approximately $120,000 in pledges were raised.

The City of Nampa cooperated in supporting the school financially during this time period and during latter years. A 1919 report shows that Nampa residents contributed $5,885 from 1916 to 1918. In 1923, the city pledged itself to raise $10,000 for the school in a year.

Material donations were also welcome. The Nampa Chamber of Commerce provided the school with a carload of precious coal during the winter of 1924. In the spring of 1924, the Nampa D department store forgave a promissory note for $662.53 on which the accrued interest amounted to $152.35.

The students had their own way of holding down the costs. They organized a Students' Club in 1916 in order to provide meals for boarding students at the lowest possible cost. By hiring a cook and doing the rest of the work themselves, the students kept the price of food down to an average of five cents per meal. "Later, when war times came on, the price was raised to seven cents;" and when balancing the budget necessitated another half cent raise, the students were indignant.

But by 1918 the students had another worry. When the Spanish influenza swept westward in October, community leaders ordered N.N.C., along with all other schools, to discontinue work. Instead, the school continued operation under a strict quarantine with most of the students and faculty living in the dormitories. "The

This early picture of the N.N.C. campus shows two of the first buildings on campus. (ISHS)

only connection with the outside was "Dad" Wines and his little wagon that he hauled up and down the sidewalk, to and from town, with the necessary supplies."

The campus did not remain immune from the epidemic, however. Once the flu struck, the dormitories were in essence turned into hospitals. Dr. Mangum, who had just arrived on campus, supervised about twenty-five of the older students who gave nursing care to the sick. Approximately 200 students contracted the flu and yet no one died. Once the worst of the epidemic was over on campus students were sent home for a period of recuperation and the school was closed. Classwork began again after the beginning of the New Year in 1919. But because of the flu epidemic, "the institution was almost ruined financially."

By the end of 1926, "the College enrollment had grown from six to one hundred and eight." In addition, ninety-two students had received degrees from the College of Liberal Arts and more than one hundred had graduated from the Academy. In the fall of 1926 Rev. Russell Victor DeLong came to the school as a professor of philosophy and theology and in the spring of 1927 became first acting president and then president of the institution.

When he took over the administration of the college, President DeLong faced an indebtedness of $93,000 upon the school. The interest on the debt alone amounted to over $20,000 and "the institution in reality was in the hands of a receiver, for the Nampa Investment Corporation had been made trustee, and all business was transacted through this corporation, so that the current funds would not be in jeopardy." Most of the debt was caused by capital obligations but faculty members had not been paid in full for their salaries for several years.

In April of 1927 President DeLong launched an "Out-of-Debt Campaign" with the understanding that if enough money could not be raised to wipe out the entire indebtedness, the college would be closed. Subscriptions began with the faculty and student body and in the first day $13,000 was promised.

During the ensuing months, district assemblies, churches, conventions and individuals were approached to support the college.

Bit by bit the total climbed until by February of 1928 only $15,000 was left to be raised. This amount was not to come easily, however, because the supporters of N.N.C. had been saturated with fund raising appeals.

In the fall of 1928 the finance committee set November 1 as the "zero hour" when either the entire indebtedness was to be wiped out or the college would close its doors. An intense fund-raising effort was undertaken during the month proceeding this deadline. But "Wednesday evening, the night before November 1, the committee lacked $5000 of having sufficient to cover the entire indebtedness."

That night the finance committee sent out more than a hundred telegrams to churches and individuals. By the next morning, N.N.C. supporters promised payment of the remaining balance. On November 28th, the college wrote checks to cover all of its debts. After a twenty month campaign, the institution balanced its books and stood free and clear financially.

The payment of the debt caused increased confidence in the school and consequently the enrollment increased over fifty per cent in September of 1929. This, in turn, caused crowded conditions which necessitated consideration of a building program on campus. Hesitant, however, to commit large sums of money, the Board of Regents agreed on a plan to remodel and enlarge the administration building and to raise the money for this project by selling bricks for a dollar a piece. The money raised was used to buy sand and cement and student labor made the cement bricks. The goal was to make 300,000 bricks. The college bought a cement machine and "during the college year, different shifts of young men were employed each school day and on Saturdays."

This effort was a start, but after two years the proposed expansion was not yet underway. Therefore, the Board agreed to take out a loan for $30,000 with the Home Building and Loan Association of Nampa which consented to amortize the loan on a ten year basis. During the summer of 1931 the college hired S.W. True as contractor and the remodeling and enlargement of the administration building began.

At the same time the school felt a tremendous need for a physical education building. After working out a plan to have this structure financed by payments from the Idaho-Oregon district camp meeting and a fee paid by the student body, the school went ahead with construction of a new gym. In the end, money from the loan taken out for remodeling of the administration building was

Professor C. V. Marshall directs this science lab at N.N.C. in the early 1930s. Marshall taught at the school from 1914 to 1936 and started the first science department at the college. (Courtesy, N.N.C.)

By 1932 the administration building has been enlarged and bricked and several other buildings have been added to the campus. (ISHS)

sufficient to cover the costs of completing the physical education building as well.

By the time the 1932 school year opened, the nation and the college felt severely the impact of the Depression. Early in the school year, the school introduced the transfer system whereby the faculty received services or goods in lieu of cash payments for their salaries. Most of the faculty moved into the dormitories and received room and board on transfer. For those who remained outside the dormitories, "'pay' consisted of $5.00 a month, which was given with the understanding that it was to cover light and water bills first."

The college received many food items on transfer, including honey, flour, popcorn, apples, potatoes, tomatoes, onions, carrots, turnips, parsnips, winter celery and head lettuce. Spices, soap, medicines, cereal, milk, and butter also became part of the transfer trade. Because of a shortage of meat and eggs, "eggless cakes" and "meatless dishes" became popular.

Sagebrush was the only fuel freely available, but it required constant work to keep a sagebrush fire going. It also took at least one hour to chop enough sagebrush to keep a fire burning for a day.

By February of 1933, only two faculty families lived outside the dormitories but that month seemed to be a turning point. Some money began to come into the school and "by the end of the school year, the faculty had received from $125 to $150 each in cash."

In the summer of 1935 Dr. DeLong was recalled to the

presidency of N.N.C. Again he faced a financial crisis. During the depression, monthly payments were not met on the loan taken out to remodel the administration building and build the gym and the mortgage company was threatening to foreclose. Dr. DeLong sent out an appeal to N.N.C.'s constituents and $5000 was raised which was sufficient to prevent the sale of the property.

Dr. DeLong was also convinced that a plan for regular financial support was needed by the college rather than continually sending out emergency appeals. Thus, the Board of Regents adopted a proposal asking each district to include an education budget in its financial plans. The districts agreed to this proposal.

Following Dr. DeLong's second administration, the school weathered the problems caused by World War II and the post-war period under the administration of President Lewis T. Corlett. In 1952, Dr. John E. Riley moved from the position of pastor of College Church in Nampa to president of the institution. During his tenure in office, numerous changes occurred at the school.

From 1952 to 1972, student enrollment increased from 485 to 1007. The faculty positions grew from thirty-two to seventy-four with approximately forty per cent of the faculty holding earned doctorates. The library increased its holdings from 15,500 volumes to 84,000 and moved into a new facility.

During this same time period an extensive building program was undertaken with financing arranged through United States government loans. In 1952, the gross assets of the college were valued at approximately one million dollars. In 1973, the college owned assets valued at nine and a half million "with net worth growing from $600,000 to upwards of six million."

During Dr. Riley's tenure as president of the college, the school emphasized a firm commitment to academic achievement. Dr.

Dr. John E. Riley served as president of N.N.C. from 1952 to 1972, a time of great growth and expansion for the school. (Courtesy, N.N.C.)

The administration building, shown here in the 1950s, serves as the center of the Northwest Nazarene College campus. (ISHS)

EARLY CHURCHES IN NAMPA

The Nampa Christian Church started in this tabernacle built in 1906, at Fourth Street and "H" Street, later named Thirteenth Avenue. In 1910, the church built a new struc- ture at the same location. (Courtesy, Frances Coyle)

The Grace Episcopal Church was located at Twelfth Avenue and Third Street South in 1910. (ISHS)

The Church of the Brethren was built in 1901 at Eleventh Avenue and Third Street South. J. H. Graybill who came to Nampa from Roanoke, Virginia, served as the first pastor. This building was replaced by a new church which opened in January of 1938 at Eleventh Avenue and Fourth Street South. (Courtesy, Carl Martin)

Below: The Methodist Church, built in 1902 at the corner of Twelfth Avenue and Fourth Street South, cost $3500. It was remodeled in 1923. (CCHS)

The Friends Church, started in Nampa in 1935, occupied this building, located at Thirteenth Avenue and Eighth Street South. The church building had previously been used by the Mennonites and by N.N.C. during the school's first year. (Courtesy, Hazel Antrim)

The Catholic Church was built in Nampa before the turn of the century. (CCHS)

St. Paul's Catholic Church, built in 1910, was located at Eighth Street and Fifteenth Avenue South. (ISHS)

The interior of St. Paul's is shown in this photo. (ISHS)

Dr. Thelma B. Culver was academic dean of the college from 1946 to 1970. (Courtesy, Helen Wilson)

The John E. Riley Library was built on the N.N.C. campus in the 1960's. (Photo by Jim Thomas)

Thelma Culver encouraged this emphasis while she was academic dean of the college from 1946 to 1970. In 1967, the school received accreditation of its teacher education program from the National Council for the Accreditation of Teacher Education. At the time, N.N.C. was one of the few schools in Idaho to receive this distinction and one of the rare small, church-related liberal arts colleges in the nation to be acknowledged by NCATE.

In 1971, John Luik became N.N.C.'s first Rhodes Scholar, receiving a scholarship to study at the University of Oxford in England for two years. The school's academic strength was again acknowledged in 1984 when Ginger Rinkenberger became N.N.C.'s second Rhodes Scholar.

Kenneth Pearsall and Gordon Wetmore followed Dr. Riley as presidents of N.N.C. in the 1970s and 80s. In recent years the school continues to be concerned about financial support and student enrollment, especially as government sponsored student loans decrease. However, the school remains closely aligned with its Nazarene constituency, serving the educational needs of its youth, and has grown to be a vital element in the town of Nampa.

IDAHO STATE SCHOOL AND HOSPITAL

In March of 1911 the Idaho Legislature passed a bill providing for the establishment of an Idaho State Sanitarium for feeble-minded and epileptic people. The bill contained an appropriation of $25,000 for the purchase of a site and construction of a building and a provision requiring that the institution be located within twenty miles of the state capital.

By May the commission entrusted with selecting the site for the new state institution was investigating over twenty locations that

had been proposed within the twenty mile limit. After a few days they narrowed the choice to two --- a Nampa site and one near Meridian. The commission chose the Nampa location when Nampa offered to purchase for the state forty acres of the eighty-acre site and to reduce the price on the other forty acres from $140 to $125 per acre. Thus, the state acquired the eighty acre location for $5000.

On the day of the selection of the site Governor Hawley expressed some of his plans and philosophy for the institution. Although he expected it to be the "greatest institution in the state," he anticipated that the state would spend as little money as possible for its maintenance. "An institution of this kind must be made self-sustaining as near as possible," he asserted, and the way to accomplish this goal, according to the governor, was to engage the residents of the institution in farm labor.

Furthermore, he thought that even if the financial condition of the state did not dictate the self-sufficiency of such an institution, the residents should be organized into a work force for their own benefit. Seeing some inherent advantage in farm work, the governor noted, "the welfare of the unfortunates detained there requires that they be in the open air and perform more or less labor." Eventually, the governor envisioned a 2000-acre farm operation which would produce the meat and produce used at the institution as well as cash crops such as sugar beets, grain and hay.

By March of 1912, a year after the initial appropriation for the institution was passed by the legislature, work had begun on the Idaho State Sanitarium. The Board of Directors awarded the Nampa Lumber Company a contract for $1650 for lumber for the building and prisoners from the state penitentiary cleared the land and prepared the ground for construction. Dr. J. W. Givens from the Board of Directors anticipated that the project would be completed by March of 1913.

He was unduly optimistic. Insufficient funding from the state

The state legislature founded the Idaho State School and Hopital in 1911, calling it the State Sanitarium, but legislators did not appropriate enough money to open the facility until 1918. (Courtesy, Elaine Chapin)

HEALTH CARE IN EARLY NAMPA

Dr. J. H. Murray, one of Nampa's earliest physicians, came to the town in 1890. He lived to be 102 years old. (CCHS)

The McLain Hardware store, located at 1302 First Street South, housed Nampa's first hospital on its second floor in the town's early days. (CCHS)

Dr. Hugh Prescott Ross who practiced in Nampa in the early twentieth century, was instrumental in establishing Mercy Hospital. (CCHS)

Mercy Hospital opened on November 9, 1919. The facility was built through a joint effort of the community, the Catholic Church, and the Sisters of Mercy. (ISHS)

slowed work on the institution for several years.   In 1915 Governor Moses Alexander vetoed an appropriation bill which would have provided funds for the completion of the sanitarium. When the Nampa Chamber of Commerce invited him to visit the site and explain his lack of support for the project, he contended that the institution should never have been started in the first place. The legislature did appropriate $4000 that year to maintain the grounds and care for what had been done, but it was 1917 before an intensive lobbying effort by a number of Idaho women succeeded in getting the legislature and governor to appropriate sufficient funds for the completion of the building.

In June of 1918 the institution opened with forty patients who were moved from Idaho's two state mental hospitals. These people were not mentally ill but had been housed at the mental hospitals because there was no other place for them.   The newspaper announced that there was room for twenty more residents. Initially, the sanitarium accepted residents with varying degrees of mental retardation: borderline, mild, moderate, severe and profound. Many of the people were ambulatory and, thus, two story buildings were constructed.

Once the Idaho State Sanitarium was opened in 1918, it continued to grow. In 1919, two wings were added to Whitehall, the institution's only building at that time. (Courtesy, Elaine Chapin)

Once the institution was opened, it continued to grow. In 1919 and 1920 the daily population averaged ninety. The annual cost of maintenance per resident was approximately $375. In 1919 two wings were added to Whitehall, the institution's only building, to help accommodate the growing number of residents.

From 1926 to 1932 the population of the institution increased from approximately 280 residents to 470 and some construction was undertaken in order to provide sufficient housing. The institution also underwent a name change during this time period, changing from "Idaho State Sanitarium" to "State School and Colony for the Feebleminded and Epileptic."

In 1935 the state purchased additional ground for the institution, bringing the total number of acres to 581. The school continued to be overcrowded, however, until two additional residential units were built in 1938.

Also the institution lacked sufficient professional services in the 1930s. The superintendent was the only physician on staff. The total staff numbered only thirty-six people for nearly 500 residents in 1937.   A staff person on a ward was paid $50 a month, supervisors were paid $65 a month, and fifteen members of the payroll received five dollars a week. In 1939 the staff worked twelve-hour days.

The overcrowding and lack of professional staff may have contributed to the epidemics which were common during these days. In 1935, at one time 200 residents had scarlet fever. There was also an outbreak of influenza and mumps during that same year.

In the 1920s and 1930s the residents helped to support the institution by operating the farm. Consequently, little effort was made to move residents out of the institution and escapes were common. In 1933-34, for example, six residents escaped from the institution.

When a consulting psychologist was hired in 1939 for a two-month period to do psychological evaluations, the results indicated that some residents did not need institutional care and may not have even been developmentally disabled. Some children were found to be functioning at a dull-normal level and may have been entirely normal had they not been in an institutional environment since infancy.

In 1940 organized athletics and music activities were begun on the campus along with vocational training which provided items of benefit to the institution. From 1940 to 1950 the population of the school increased from 550 residents to 710. The budget increased from approximately $72,000 in 1940 to $216,209 in 1949.

After the institution reached a peak population of over 900 residents in 1956, a move began in the late 1950s and early 1960s to place the most capable residents into the community. (Courtesy, Elaine Chapin)

The 1950s appear to be a turning point for the institution. In 1952 the Ramsey Training Center was opened and the institution began to function with the help of professional staff. In 1957 the first full-time social worker was hired and in 1960 a full-time physician, Dr. Clarence A. McIntyre, was added. In that same year, Dr. Erwin Sage, a physician who had retired from the Department of Health in San Francisco, came to the State School as the Superintendent of the Institution. Dr. McIntyre and Dr. Sage put together a comprehensive medical care program for the patients with consultants in neurology, cardiology and general medical practice. Under their supervision the State School and Hospital attracted a number of medical school students and pharmacological trainees who came to I.S.S.H. for internships.

After the institution reached a peak population of over 900 in 1956, a move began in the late 1950s and early 1960s to place the most capable residents into the community. As a part of this

Governor Robert Smylie spoke at the dedication of the gymnasium at the Idaho State School in the late 1950s. (ISHS)

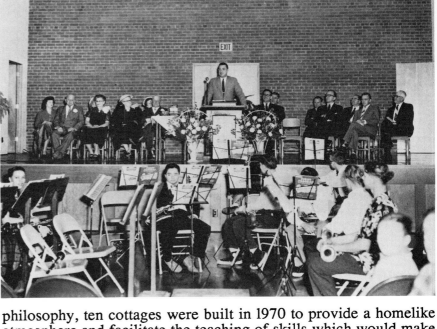

philosophy, ten cottages were built in 1970 to provide a homelike atmosphere and facilitate the teaching of skills which would make the residents capable of functioning outside of the institution. From July of 1971 to May of 1976, 196 residents were placed into the community.

Currently called the Idaho State School and Hospital, the institution functions with a vastly different composition of people on campus. The population has decreased to approximately 320 residents but the budget has increased because of the severity of mental retardation of these residents. Thirty-eight percent require skilled nursing care and sixty percent have no understandable speech. The institution cares for those who cannot be served by other facilities, yet continues an emphasis on educational and training programs tailored to fit the needs of the severely handicapped. Also, evaluation and treatment by the medical staff is augmented by the utilization of specialists when needed.

Perhaps the change in the institution is symbolized by the attitude toward farm labor which was thought so vital when the sanitarium first opened. In 1939 and 1940 over $54,000 of farm products were raised at the institution with resident labor. Recently, the farm services and facilities were re-evaluated with the conclusion being that they were not economically feasible or useful for vocational training because of the small number of residents capable of being involved in this type of activity.

Currently, the Idaho State School and Hospital serves approximately 320 residents who require specialized care which cannot be provided elsewhere in the state. (Photo by Jim Thomas)

EARLY NAMPA SCHOOLS

Students pose in front of Lakeview School in 1898 before the new school was built. Lakeview was Nampa's first school building. (CCHS)

This vehicle served as Nampa's first school "bus." (CCHS)

Kenwood School was built in 1901. (ISHS, Courtesy, Dr. Raymond J. Bungard)

The first addition to Kenwood School was constructed in 1907. A second wing, added a couple of years later, further enlarged the space available at the school. (ISHS)

These school children attended Lone Tree School near Nampa at the time this picture was taken in March of 1909. (ISHS)

The sophomore class at Nampa High School in 1911 included: back row, left to right -- Hazel Hartley, Alfreda Hansen, Anna Roosma, LeRoy Grass, Ralph King, Helen Hickey, and Tilden Lockman. Middle row, from left -- Ruth Patterson, Austin Babcock, Grace Philpot, Maybell Thomas, Winette Wing, Maggie Anderson, Emma Anketell. Front row, left to right -- Dora MacPherson, True Potter, Grover Everett, Naomi Pember, Joyce Jenness, Donald Lamson, Mary Criner, Thelda Horne, and Geraldine Dewey. (ISHS)

The Nampa High School band is shown here in 1912. (CCHS)

The Nampa High School football team in 1912 included: Back row -- Earl Garrity, Tilden Lockman, Frank Joyner, Ronald Everely, and Mr. Herbert T. Niece. Front row -- John Hatfield, LeRoy Grass, Art Egbert, Clifford McNary, Grimes, Larson, and Frank Terry. (Courtesy, Lucy Redmon)

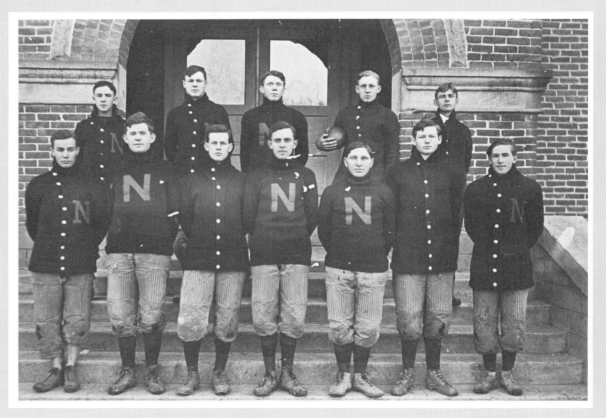

The senior girls at Nampa High School in 1914 included: from left -- Laura Miller, Lizzie Dyson, Elizabeth Waigand, Vera Heilig, Eva Hamilton, Eleanor Lamson, Edith Hays, Harriet Anketell, Vivian Amoureaux, and Viola Thompson. (ISHS)

The Nampa Senior High School first opened for classes in the fall of 1917. B. R. Riordan served as the first principal of the new facility. It became a junior high school when the new high school opened on Lake Lowell Avenue in 1955. The old senior high school building was razed in the 1970s. (Courtesy, Elaine Chapin)

V
World War I and the 1920s:
1917 - 1929

Long before the United States entered the "war to end all wars," Nampans began to anticipate participation in the conflict that was eventually to become world-wide. In April of 1914, the Leader-Herald reported:

> Company B, Nampa's organization in the national guards, has not yet marched down the street shouting its readiness, amid a bluster of trumpets and hot air, to go to war. But in a quiet, earnest and patriotic spirit the local boys are discussing their part in the drama that is being staged --- possibly to change world history.

Three years later, Nampa's unit of the Idaho National Guard

F. G. Cottingham and Win Nettleton constructed this building around 1890 at the corner of Eleventh Avenue and Front Street South. It was referred to as the Armory because it was used for several years by Nampa's Battery B. (Courtesy, Jerry Cornilles)

Facing Page: The railroad continued to connect Nampa to the rest of the world in the days of World War I and after. The women in this picture are typical of the "new woman" of the 1920s. During that decade, women bobbed their hair, shortened their skirts and faced the world with a new image. (CCHS)

received orders to mobilize. On March 26, 1917, Captain George H. van de Steeg, commander of Nampa's Company B, began rounding up his men at the local armory and preparing them to take to the field in response to orders from the War Department which were sent to Idaho Governor Moses Alexander.

But movement out of town was delayed until additional recruits could be added to Nampa's unit. Eighty men belonged to Company B when mobilization began. A few days after the mobilization order was received, recruiters began an "aggressive campaign" to increase the company's size to 150 men, the number set by the adjutant general to bring the guard company up to "war strength."

By April 3, 1917, the day after President Woodrow Wilson addressed a special session of the United States Congress, asking it to declare war on Germany, Nampa's guard unit numbered ninety-four men. Local officers anticipated orders to move into Boise when the company's strength reached one-hundred. In preparation for mobilization, Nampa's guards were drilling about five hours a day, three hours in the morning and two in the afternoon. Most members of the company were allowed to go home each evening, but some stayed to guard the armory.

Eventually Nampa's Company B received orders for St. Maries, in northern Idaho, and then went to the East Coast. Here the company mobilized, increased their equipment, and departed for France where the company served as a field artillery unit. After the armistice, Nampa's Company B was stationed in Koblenz, Germany, as part of the Army of Occupation. They returned to Nampa in July of 1919.

Nampans supported the war effort, as did communities across

Nampa prospered and grew at the end of the second decade of the twentieth century. This scene of downtown Nampa was taken sometime before 1919. (Courtesy, Winston Goering)

the nation, in a number of ways. Before Nampa's sons in Company B ever left Idaho, the Ladies Auxiliary of Company B was active, requesting donations of reading material to be sent to the boys in St. Maries.

In June of 1917, the Woman's Century Club initiated the formation of a local Red Cross chapter with a hundred people displaying some interest in the organization at their first meeting. Immediately, Mrs. Hamaker, the new president of the group, noted that the members of the Red Cross had their work cut out for them. She called attention to the need for cotton bandages at the front, their being "so scarce that newspapers have been used to staunch the flow of blood from wounds."

A few weeks later 800 people attended a meeting at the Nampa Opera House launching a Red Cross subscription fund-raising drive. Within two days, the Leader-Herald reported that the drive was progressing well with $7000 raised in the city alone. Nampa's quota was set at $7500. A caravan of fifteen automobiles drove into the country to encourage farmers' donations and the sponsors of the money-raising campaign hoped for the Nampa district to turn over $8000 to $9000 to the Red Cross.

By May of 1917, Nampa was also participating in the nation-wide Liberty Bond drive. The purchase of Liberty Bonds was encouraged as an expression of patriotism. The Leader-Herald noted, "It is up to the people to finance the war and all who can do so should hasten to buy a Liberty Bond and help Uncle Sam win a victory." Mayor Robert A. Davis Jr. pledged that he personally would match every bond purchase made in Nampa up to $500 in a single subscription.

June 5, 1917, was set aside as "registration day." On that day the banks in town closed for regular business but remained open solely for the purpose of selling Liberty Bonds. Even local businesses joined in the effort by advertising that they would take Liberty Bonds the same as cash for payment at their stores.

The war raised a variety of emotions among Nampa citizens. On April 6, 1917, the day that the U. S. House of Representatives passed a resolution recognizing the existence of a state of war with Germany making the country officially at war, Nampans joined in a rally to show their approval of the administration's stand. The newspaper reported that 1200 people marched in a parade and over 2000 people assembled to hear patriotic speeches, making the event one that "surpassed any public affair ever attempted here for enthusiasm and general participation."

Young and old joined in. The Leader-Herald caught the spirit of the event:

> 'Tommy, wave your flag, we're goin' to war.'
>
> A little blonde haired girl, a baby almost, spoke imperiously to the plump, pink faced, tired urchin beside her. She was determined that his spirits should not lag and looked at him reproachfully with a face animated by its first thrill of patriotism. Tommy stiffened with a jerk, raised his chubby arms above his head, and waved valiantly. About him hundreds of other school kiddies were doing

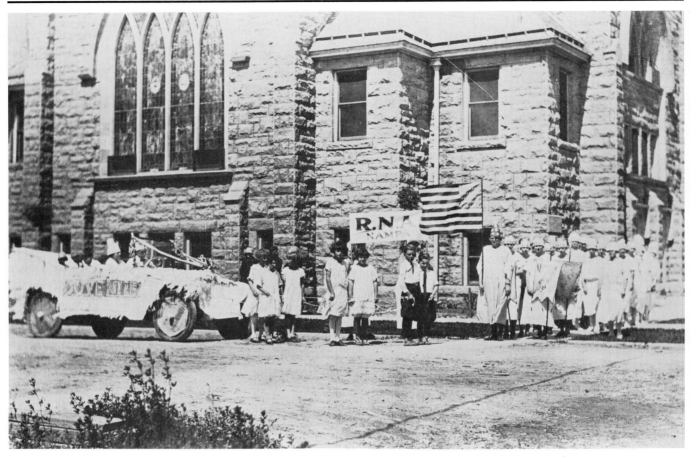

During the years of World War I, Nampans expressed their enthusiasm for the war effort through several parades staged in downtown Nampa. This picture was taken by the Presbyterian Church on Fifteenth Avenue South. (CCHS)

likewise. They were enjoying their first big emotion. They scarcely knew what caused it --- they could not know --- but some instinct, something, told them it was a big occasion and they blazed with the importance of it. They were proud to be a part of it.

Likewise, the old men felt a surge of excitement:

> The band struck up a patriotic march. The old man raised his flag tenderly, grasping its staff as tightly as though he held the most precious burden in the world, which he knew he did. He turned and glanced proudly down the line of other old men who were to march with him. . . . They knew what all this excitement meant. Patriotism was not a new emotion to them, but it was none the less warm for that.

And, at the back of the parade moved another segment of the population.

> An olive drab object swung along in the rear of the old soldiers. It moved slowly, evenly, like some perfect running machine. It, too, was soldiers --- young soldiers --- carefree boys, yet to experience the baptism of blood

but proud in the thought, they will meet it without faltering whenever it may come.

About six weeks later another rally was held in Nampa. This time patriotic music and speeches were heard by Nampa citizens on the lawn of the Dewey Palace. The purpose of the rally was to encourage enlistments in the regular army. Although a speaker named Silas Wilson, himself a veteran of the Civil War, called for unity in support of the war, his speech was interrupted by a man who carried a placard which contained a picture of Christ and the inscription, "Thou shalt not kill." The protester was not well received at the patriotic rally, but he was not alone in Nampa as a dissenter to the war effort.

Before the war started, Nampa had a local group of peace advocates which met regularly. Speaking at their February, 1917, meeting, Rev. Gates E. M. Young, pastor of Nampa's First Presbyterian Church, blamed the press for rousing emotions which might lead the United States into the European war. Contending that the European conflict was simply a commercial war between England and Germany, Rev. Young cautioned against the United States being pulled into it by those who "traffic in the word 'patriotism' but become traitors to the interests of humanity."

By the time that the United States did enter the war, the debate was spirited in the Nampa Ministerial Association over whether or not the war was morally justified. Rev. E. B. Meredith, pastor of the Baptist Church, attacked the position of the pacifist with the claim that "war has its origin in heaven." Even "aggressive warfare" is sanctioned by the Bible, declared the minister, because "war advances civilization; paves the way for freedom." Reverend Meredith had no patience with those who disagreed with him, strongly condemning those who spoke out for peace.

But that did not stop Meredith's colleagues from dissenting. At the same meeting at which the Baptist pastor spoke, Reverend William Vimont, pastor of the Methodist churches at Midway and Southside Boulevard, said it was inconsistent for Christians to go to war. "The New Testament does not in a single instance uphold war," he noted. Furthermore, he declared that Christians have a duty to die as martyrs rather than to offer resistance.

The debate spread into the community and divided the town. Years later, Nampa resident John Brandt recalled:

> I was too young to be involved directly but some of my friends were. Many of them actually volunteered. They were going to make the world safe for democracy. Kaiser Bill was a demon and so on. There was a lot of "whoop-la," songs and bands. Many of the people who went and many of the parents felt that it was not only their duty, but that they were on somewhat of a crusade.

But the Brandt family did not endorse the noble cause. John remembered:

> My dad was violently opposed to war and that may have been why I became so. ... Dad was so disturbed by the war that when the minister of the Baptist church preached that

Ben Waigand wasn't quite seventeen years old when the United States entered the war in Europe. He recalled that those of German descent were looked upon with suspicion, but loyally served their country. Here's his story:

U. S. citizens of German birth and Americans born of German parents in Nampa during the First World War were looked on unjustly, with suspicion. My father had relatives in Germany but when the United States declared war on Germany he was among the first to buy War Bonds. When I became old enough to join the Navy he was ready to sign my release. The United States government reclaimed the bonds after the war, all these bonds that they bought, after the war with Germany was over. Father took the money and bought a new car. He bought me a new car, a Chevrolet, the most modern thing then, and he bought a bunch of furniture for the kids, us kids, and a hand wind-up phonograph with a bunch of records. We sure had a lot of fun with that.

****

Several boys of German descent joined the various branches of the United States military. Bill Winter --- this was a very close friend of mine --- he and I were wireless buddies together and he joined the Signal Corps. Bill Winter was born of German parents. Both of his parents were German and couldn't hardly speak English --- wonderful mechanics. He joined the Signal Corps. He was going to Nampa High School and quit to join. I tried to join with him but was turned down. You had to be twenty-one years old to be in the service at that time. Bill made it because he was older, he was twenty-one. I wasn't quite eighteen. He was killed in action. I don't remember just where but he was killed in Germany. He was killed after they entered Germany, in action.

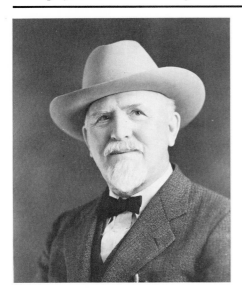

H. H. Keim served as mayor of Nampa from 1919 to 1921. (Courtesy, Margaret Goering)

this was a worthy cause, he quit going to church because of it, My mother continued to gfo and took us kids, bit Dad said that's not the Christian religion at all and if that is what they are going to teach, he was not going to church. Whether that was right or wrong, it is still evidence to the fact that there were some people who felt that this war was not justifiable.

Even after the war was over, the issue still divided the community. In April of 1919, H. H. Keim, a lay minister in the Brethren Church and a well established businessman in Nampa, was elected mayor of the town. During his tenure in office he welcomed the second annual convention of the Nonpartisan League to Nampa. In this speech, Keim said:

> I have always been opposed to war. I believe it is not the mission of Christians to fight. War permits a man to slay his brother. During the war I was subjected to criticism for these beliefs, but I kept my mouth shut because it was wise for me to do so. Some of my good friends have been imprisoned, some are still in prison, simply because they stood up for what they believed was right.

The Mayor's speech caused a flurry of protest. The Leader-Herald was shocked at Keim's "astonishing language" and confession of sympathy for those jailed for disloyalty during World War I.

The Nampa post of the Grand Army of the Republic, a veterans organization for those who fought in the Civil War, and the Nampa post of the American Legion both called for the mayor's resignation. The American Legion passed a resolution expressing "shame and disgrace" at having a "disloyal" and "unpatriotic" citizen hold the office of mayor.

Keim responded with vigor, making no apologies for his pacifist beliefs. "My life is an open book," he stated. "I have no history of word or deed that I am ashamed of. I have fixed religious convictions founded upon the principles of peace, temperance and the simple life. I have no apologies for my conduct since occupying the office of mayor, nor before." Furthermore, Keim assured his friends that he would not resign from the office of mayor.

Keim served out his term as mayor and did not run for reelection in April of 1921, but even after he left office he continued to be a center of controversy because of his anti-war beliefs. On June 12, 1921, Keim gave a religious address on a Sunday evening at a rural schoolhouse near Caldwell. In his sermon, he supported "immediate and absolute disarmament," finding the cost of war to be exorbitant. Furthermore, he criticized the Liberty Bond program which was used to finance World War I. Following the meeting, Keim circulated petitions calling upon the Idaho congressional delegation to sponsor a disarmament program.

Once again, the American Legion found his remarks highly offensive. Not only did they disagree with Keim's position, but they called him a "menace to our community" and proposed that he

H. H. Keim operated the Cold Storage Market which was located across from the Dewey Palace on First Street in downtown Nampa. (Courtesy, Margaret Goering)

"should not be allowed to live within the boundaries of the United States and should be deported along with his comrades, Bill Haywood, Emma Goldman, and others." The Grand Army of the Republic followed suit in condemning Keim and challenged the people of the town to ostracize him as a member of the community.

Keim did not sit by idly. He hired private counsel and in June of 1923 brought a $25,000 libel suit against Jenness and Son, publishers of the Nampa Leader-Herald, for inaccurate newspaper reports on his Canyon schoolhouse speech. Claiming to have lost $25,000 in his butcher business as a result of prejudicial articles published in the press, Keim also contended that he was threatened with bodily harm.

The defendants attempted to show that the published reports of Keim's speech were in essence correct. Furthermore, the Jennesses carried into the courtroom their accusations against Keim's loyalty to the country. When the trial ended after several days of testimony, the jury deliberated four hours before returning a verdict in favor of the Jennesses. The jury was not unanimous, but the verdict was

Idaho's Second Infantry unit, shown here on drill around 1917, included men from Nampa and Canyon County. (CCHS)

**Nampa Casualties
in World War I included:**

George W. Ackley
Burl Baker
Howard L. Botkin
Claude Cunningham
Oscar W. Dace
William E. Emerson
Paul J. Lockman
Harrison D. McDowell
Joseph Howard Murray, Jr.
Ray Earl Peebler
James B. Rainwater
James L. Robinson
Genevra Robinson
Oscar A. Scriven
Frank M. Turion
William J. Winter

signed by eleven of the twelve jurors, whereas nine jurors were sufficient to reach a decision in the civil suit. Keim had not proven his charges that he had been libeled.

But even those who disagreed with the war effort were sympathetic toward the Nampa boys who were fighting the war. H. H. Keim was a strong pacifist, yet two of his sons and four of his nephews served in the army during the war. In support of them, Keim bought Liberty Bonds and supported the Red Cross and the Nampa Company B Auxiliary.

Although Herman Brandt opposed the war, he sent each Nampa boy who went to fight a letter and some money. When some of them didn't return, he took it very personally, grieving with the parents and the rest of the community.

Nampa's boys, both dead and alive, returned from the war on July 2, 1919. The newspaper reported that 10,000 people joined in the combined Fourth of July and Welcome Home festivities. Howard Hartman was six years old at the time and in later years remembered the celebration as his earliest recollection about life in Nampa:

> These men were my heroes, they were fighting --- they had come back home to get started again in life.
>
> I remember when these men got off the train and lined up on Twelfth Avenue next to the men's clothing store. I think it's called the stationery store now.
>
> Our small country town had a depot in the dead end street --- still there. We all lined up on the north side of Twelfth Avenue, the dead end street, and watched the soldiers march off the train in a single file and form four abreast in the middle of the street. I loved the khaki-wrapped leggings around their legs, as they marched down the street in a straight file and column and held their tired bodies very erect. They were the lucky ones to return at all.
>
> The townspeople threw confetti and whistled and shouted til I almost went deaf. Behind the soldiers came the coffins, carried by the soldiers, and the dead killed just before the armistice was signed, or maybe after. Some were sons of prominent businessmen of our town. Women fainted and lay on the street with their eyeballs turned back up on their eyelids. Men ran to their assistance, and the soldiers marched up the street, and the coffins followed as they went north, one block, and turned east on Eleventh Avenue, and headed towards our cemetery. They marched two miles to the cemetery and entered under the arch.
>
> The soldiers formed a square and fired a salute

to the dead. The preacher made a speech and more women keeled over and fainted on the grass. The bugler blew "Taps" and more women fainted. The preacher continued his preaching about the boys coming home to return to civilian life. He told of the boys who would never return and more women fainted.

Displaying the flag of the Idaho Second Infantry Division, this soldier, along with numerous other men, fought for their country during the days of World War I. (CCHS)

NAMPA IN THE 1920'S

Americans were attempting to normalize conditions in the country following World War I. Yet the mood of the United States was vastly different from the early days of the twentieth century. Nationwide prohibition set the stage for a major experiment in social control with the implementation of the Eighteenth Amendment in January of 1920. Women became increasingly aware of their own ambitions and abilities as they began to expand their role outside of the home. They participated in the political process for the first time nationwide when the country ratified the Nineteenth Amendment in August of 1920, giving women the right to vote.

Neither prohibition nor women's suffrage were new to the Nampa community. The county outlawed alcoholic beverages in 1910 when the local option law went into effect. However, ten years later when prohibition went into effect across the country, the town expressed greater support for the experiment.

Women had been voting in Nampa since 1890 when the state constitution gave women this right. Yet in the 1920's women in Nampa showed a greater awareness of their influence not only in the political world but also in the economic and business spheres of life.

The 1920's are nostalgically remembered as the Jazz Age, but everyone did not endorse the more "permissive" behavior. Reverend Martin Damer, rector of Grace Episcopal Church, assured the town in February of 1920 that jazz music or dancing would not be permitted at the Parish Hall. However, the big controversy in Nampa in the early 1920's was whether the movie theaters would be allowed to continue to stay open on Sundays.

The automobile era had come of age in Nampa in the early 1920's. (ISHS)

The Nampa Department Store, located at 1307 First Street South, was a major retail enterprise in downtown Nampa. It was also known as the Nampa "D". (ISHS)

The Nampa Department Store changed names several times. It was known at one time as the Golden Rule Store. Later C. C. Anderson's Department Store took over the business. (ISHS)

Quinter Harris, at the center of the picture, is shown in the first Skaggs Grocery Store in Nampa around 1920. (ISHS)

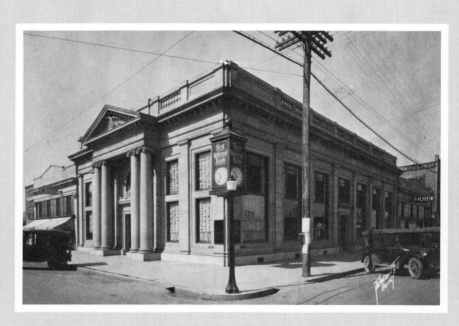

The First National Bank building at 101 Eleventh Avenue South was built in 1919. In 1966, the building was converted for use by the Nampa Public Library. (ISHS)

A 1926 Studebaker sits in front of the Greystone Hotel, originally known as the Share House. The hotel was established in the 1890s on Twelfth Avenue South between First and Second Streets. (CCHS)

The Forve Paint and Art Store, located at 1120 First Street South, was typical of the 1920s' commercial storefronts. (CCHS)

Earl B. Crooks opened the C-B Oil Company in Nampa in May of 1921. (Courtesy, Louis A. Reichart)

Sparks Pool Hall, located where the Greenhurst Gift Shop is now operating, provided hours of entertainment for Nampans in the 1920s. The local pool halls sold cigars, coffee and snacks during the days of prohibition. (CCHS)

This Farm and Fireside parade was held on First Street in Nampa around 1925. The meat store in the background is the Anketell Meat Company. (CCHS)

On August 11, 1924, the Ku Klux Klan held a parade on First Street in downtown Nampa. The gathering, part of an Inter-State convention held in Nampa, was noted as the largest demonstration of the Ku Klux Klan ever to be assembled in Idaho. Several thousand Klansmen from Idaho, Utah and eastern Oregon attended the convention. (ISHS)

The Pacific Fruit Express shops, which worked on railroad cars, were opened in Nampa in May of 1926. The enterprise was advertised as a million-dollar business venture at the time and encompassed eighteen buildings located on a 73-acre site. (ISHS)

The P.F.E. also included an icing plant which supplied cold storage railroad cars. The railroad-related business continued to serve as a major employer in Nampa until recent years. (ISHS)

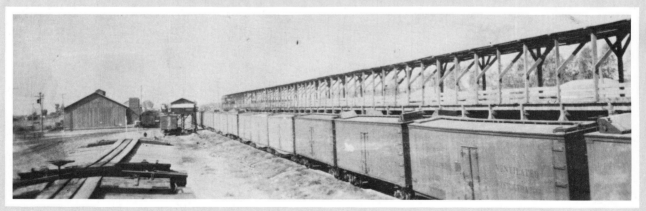

Airplanes were a new sight which caused great curiosity and excitement in the 1920s. In the fall of 1920, Leo and Orval Hostetler flew in the second plane to be seen in Nampa. (CCHS)

This baseball team was sponsored by the P.F.E. shop. The team took second place in the finals of the Union Pacific Athletic League played at Boise in August of 1928. (CCHS)

VI Agricultural Activism: 1905 - 1928

By the time Alexander Duffes took advantage of the Homestead Act to begin the town of Nampa in 1885, good agricultural ground that did not need irrigation was already settled in the West. The land around Nampa was sagebrush-covered-desert, yet Duffes envisioned the area surrounded by fertile farmlands. Not only would farming make the area self-sufficient, but marketing potential beyond the immediate town existed. Locally, the Owyhee mines in Silver City provided an outlet for farm crops, but of greater significance, the railroad furnished the possibility of developing a national market for valley produce.

Facing page: This early threshing crew in the Lone Star area south of Nampa used a steam-powered tractor. (CCHS)

Homesteaders had to remove sagebrush as large as that shown here before they could begin to cultivate the land. (CCHS)

The Phyllis Canal was one of the first attempts to bring irrigation water to the region surrounding Nampa. (Courtesy, Jerry Cornilles)

When farming began in the Nampa area, farmers used horse teams to pull plows. (ISHS)

Water was necessary to fulfill this vision. When Duffes, James McGee and James Stewart incorporated the town, they understood that bringing irrigation to the region was essential, yet they failed to foresee the difficulties of this enterprise. By the 1880s, Eastern capitalists were speculating on Western irrigation projects. Perhaps they were drawn by the romantic notion of "making the desert bloom like a rose." But when they found the return on their investment negligible, they often sold their interests to the settlers.

By the turn of the century, three canal projects were furnishing water for the Boise Valley with limited success. The New York Canal, the ambitious brainchild of A. D. Foote, the engineer who planned to bring 300,000 to 500,000 acres under irrigation, was barely functioning. The Phyllis Canal supplied water to 3737 acres in 1900. The most successful of the early irrigation systems, the

Ridenbaugh Canal, provided water for 80,000 acres at the turn of the century, with 49,000 of those acres being cultivated.

Private enterprise had done about all that it could to bring irrigation to the farms of the Boise Valley. When President Theodore Roosevelt signed the bill establishing the United States Reclamation Service in 1902, the Boise Valley offered a prime opportunity for the federal government to bring expanded irrigation to an area which had been promised water for fifteen to twenty years.

A twenty-four-horse team provided the power to run this early combine. (ISHS)

THE DEER FLAT RESERVOIR

Even before Congress passed the 1902 Reclamation Act, Idaho began anticipating a Boise Valley reclamation project by searching for water storage sites. When all the upstream storage possibilities seemed undesirable, the Boise Valley Irrigation Association which had been formed by all the major canal companies of the area, explored two locations south of Nampa at Deer Flat in November of 1902. On April 23, 1903, the Reclamation Service authorized a preliminary survey of the Payette-Boise project which included the possible development of a Deer Flat Reservoir.

After the Reclamation Service reported favorably on the Boise Valley project, supporters of the proposal held a series of meetings informing farmers of the potential development. Many of these farmers already were part of an irrigation system but suffered from an insufficient water supply. Farmers readily gave their support to the project. In January and February of 1904, the city councils of Boise, Nampa, Caldwell, Emmett, Meridian and Parma formally endorsed the proposal and three irrigation districts followed with requests that the project be funded. The State Land Board also lent its support to the plan.

Under the leadership of J. H. Lowell, the irrigators who strongly supported the reclamation project formed the Payette-Boise

Workers used a grader hauled by a traction engine in the early stage of construction of the Deer Flat Reservoir embankment in 1908. (ISHS)

Users' Association on March 4, 1904, in D. W. Ross' reclamation office in Boise. By that time, approximately 1200 farmers, owners of 94,664 acres of irrigated land, had committed themselves to participation in the government project.

But that same month, Boise Valley farmers experienced a financial setback with their plans. The Reclamation Service awarded $2,600,000, the total amount available for reclamation in the state, to a Minidoka project. However, that did not discourage those promoting the Payette-Boise project. Surveying for the potential project went right on and the Payette-Boise Water Users' Association officially incorporated September 9, 1904. It was of some help that the southwestern Idaho proposal had the support of D. W. Ross who was in charge of the Idaho office of the Reclamation Service. J. H. Lowell continued to gather support for the project until he had over 1500 land owners representing 125,736 acres signed up in support of irrigation development by the government.

In March of 1905 the work done by D. W. Ross and J. H. Lowell began to pay off. That month the director of the United States Geological Survey and the Secretary of the Interior authorized the Boise-Payette project and shifted half of the Idaho reclamation funds or $1,300,000 away from the Minidoka project to be used for

The elevating grader used to construct the Deer Flat Reservoir, dug up the ground and placed the dirt on a revolving conveyor belt which dumped it into wagons alongside the belt. (ISHS)

irrigation development in the Boise Valley. This allotment was thought to be sufficient to build two dams for the Deer Flat Reservoir, enlarge the New York Canal, and construct a small diversion dam on the Boise River.

Preliminary work included obtaining right-of-ways for the land needed for the reservoir. Area bankers appraised arid, unimproved land in the Deer Flat region at twelve to fifteen dollars an acre in an attempt to help the project get underway, but some land owners held out for more. D. E. Burley took his claim to the United States Supreme Court where he was awarded twenty dollars an acre, a price lower than that which had been offered him in earlier negotiations. Overall, the reclamation service paid $222,091 for 9620 acres of land secured for the reservoir. This averaged $23.77 per acre. Ross initially estimated that the site would cost $239,000.

The Reclamation Service solicited bids for building the Diversion Dam, enlargement of the New York Canal, and construction of the two embankments for the Deer Flat Reservoir in February of 1906. When they were opened, most were disappointingly high. Nonetheless, the Reclamation Service awarded the Utah Fire Proofing Company the contract for the Diversion Dam on February 21, 1906 with a bid of $158,950. This segment of the project was to be completed by April 1, 1907, but was plagued by delays. At least nineteen superintendents supervised this construction. In October of 1908 when the Diversion Dam was finally completed, the contractor figured that he lost $89,360 on the project.

This six-horse team drew a five-ton ridged roller to compact the earth on the embankment of the Deer Flat Reservoir. Recent examination of the embankment showed it to be almost as firm as concrete. (ISHS)

The enlargement of the New York Canal was divided into three segments with different contractors taking responsibility for each section. Work commenced on the New York Canal, by then called the "Main Canal," in May of 1906. One segment had to be completed by the Reclamation Service when the contractor seemed incapable of doing the work. The only profit earned on the New York Canal and the Diversion Dam went to the firm of Conway and Wilhite who contracted to construct the New York Canal from Indian Creek to Deer Flat. The company began work in February of 1906 and supplemented the work force with "common drunks collected by the police force of Nampa" who turned these "hobos" over to the contractors.

The bids for the Upper Embankment of the Deer Flat Reservoir

Enlargement of the New York Canal, also called the Main Canal, was part of the Deer Flat Reclamation project. (CCHS)

were rejected completely and the Reclamation Service itself took charge of this portion of the project. In order to undertake this construction, the Reclamation Service purchased two steam shovels, five locomotives, sixty dump cars, three miles of rails, 4000 railroad ties, five sprinkler wagons, and numerous other items. The workers excavated 30,000 cubic yards for the dam's foundation, then placed approximately one million yards of earth and gravel on the embankment. The embankment was seventy feet high and 5000 feet long when it was completed.

A small town sprang up at the site during the construction. Workers occupied sixteen buildings, including a mess house, four bunkhouses, a reading room, a storehouse and granary, stables, and a blacksmith shop. The mess hall contained two large ranges, hot and cold water, and enough room to accommodate 120 men. The Reclamation Service utilized American labor, giving preference to homesteaders.

The smaller Lower Embankment was constructed under the supervision of the firm of Hubbard and Carlson who had earlier worked on the Minidoka Reclamation Project. This embankment was built with approximately 928,000 cubic yards of earth and gravel. The total cost tallied $286,316, slightly less than originally estimated.

Horses moved the railroad track at the Deer Flat Reservoir. (ISHS)

By 1909, when the Diversion Dam, the enlarged New York Canal and the Deer Flat Reservoir were completed, the government had spent $2,500,000 on the project. Nampans celebrated the formal opening of the Main Canal on February 22, 1909, but shortly after expressed apprehension concerning the success of the project. When much of the water in the reservoir was lost due to seepage and evaporation after the initial filling, the Nampa Chamber of Commerce wrote the Idaho Congressional delegation with the news that "the big Deer Flat Reservoir will not hold water." Furthermore, they recommended that a new reservoir be built further up the Boise River rather than to try to salvage the Deer Flat project.

But the Deer Flat Reservoir could and did hold water. The Boise Project provided irrigation water for 10,000 acres of farmland in 1907, 15,000 acres in 1908 and an additional 18,000 acres in 1909 and 1910. After the Deer Flat Reservoir was completely finished in March of 1911, irrigated acreage in Canyon County jumped again. Whereas, the county contained less than 50,000 acres of irrigated farmland in 1900, by 1920, 200,000 acres received water. In 1900 there were approximately 800 farms in Canyon County. By 1910 this figure increased to approximately 2900.

Shown here are the New York Canal headgates. The formal opening of the enlarged New York Canal was held February 22, 1909. (CCHS)

Nampa area farmers were anxious to have the Reclamation Service develop irrigation for this region. However, once the Deer Flat Reservoir was completed, the farmers found that all of their problems had not been solved. For one thing, they were not satisfied with the repayment schedules for the Boise Project set by the Reclamation Service. Beginning in 1915, Boise Valley farmers engaged in a complicated repayment battle with the Reclamation Service.

Furthermore, local farmers accused the administrators of the Boise Project of being inefficient and incompetent. During the 1917 irrigation season, 450 Canyon County water users met in Caldwell and drafted a resolution calling for the dismissal of the officials in charge of the Boise Project because they failed to store sufficient water in the Deer Flat Reservoir to provide for the needs of the farmers dependent upon the project. The system should irrigate approximately 250,000 acres, said the farmers, yet "in the midst of the irrigation season, when the demand for irrigation water is the greatest, we, the water users of the Boise project, find, to our great injury, the Deer Flat reservoir is now practically empty." Consequently, fields of grain and alfalfa were burning up for lack of irrigation water and the farmers anticipated losing millions of dollars.

D. W. Cole, the manager of the Boise Project, failed to attend the farmers' meeting, saying that he was too busy supervising repair work on the New York Canal. The canal had ruptured twice during the early part of the irrigation season, causing one farm to be flooded with five feet of water. The first break was thought to be caused by a gopher hole.

In addition to these problems, the administrators of the Reclamation Service aggravated the farmers by failing to provide for any system wherein the farmers had a voice in the management of the irrigation projects. Some water users thought the project officials were unduly harsh in enforcing regulations.

THE NONPARTISAN LEAGUE

All of these complaints led Canyon County farmers to begin to engage in political action to try to remedy their problems. Just before the 1916 election, frustrated farmers formed the Idaho Federation of Agriculture and then successfully campaigned to elect Democrats to a majority in the state legislature for the first time since the days of Populism and free silver in the 1890s.

However, when the legislature met in January of 1917, the Democratic majority failed to listen to the wishes of the small farmers who put them into office. After some token concessions to the farmers, the legislators dealt with the problems of the mining and lumber industries and then turned their attention to legislation aimed at curbing the activities of the Industrial Workers of the World who were active in northern Idaho.

J. P. Gray maintained this Nampa packing house, shown in approximately 1910. (ISHS)

Governor Moses Alexander failed to support the Federation of Agriculture's proposal for a strong state farm marketing bureau. Then he further alienated himself from the farmers by dismissing the man they considered their main advocate in his administration, William Scholtz, director of the existing farm market bureau. In a letter written to the Nampa Leader-Herald in August of 1917, a local farmer asked why the governor had not been impeached because of his abandonment of the farmers and cattle men of Idaho who elected him. "Verily, verily, I say unto you, this is not the Moses that led the children out of the wilderness," concluded the farmer.

Discouraged with the possibilities of gaining agrarian reforms through regular political channels, Idaho farmers became interested in the activities of Arthur C. Townley and the Nonpartisan League. Organized in North Dakota by grain growers who wanted publicly-owned establishments to process and market farm products and state-operated banks to provide farmers with inexpensive credit, the Nonpartisan League promised economic justice to Idaho farmers.

Willard Deal, a Nampa area farmer who headed the Idaho State Grange, invited the Nonpartisan League into Idaho in early 1917. Ray McKaig, master of the North Dakota Grange, came to a farmers' convention in Boise in February of 1917 and spoke at length on the benefits of the Nonpartisan League. Following his address, convention delegates, visibly impressed by McKaig, voted overwhelmingly to organize a League in Idaho.

The farmers began organizing in May of 1917 with country picnics and town rallies. Orators, including W. W. Deal from Nampa, loudly promoted the League's crusade against social and economic injustice. In August of 1917, organizers estimated an enrollment of 4000 farmers in the Nonpartisan League and by 1919, the League claimed 12,000 members in Idaho.

Nampa area farmers were particularly receptive to the campaign of the Nonpartisan League. Townley encouraged his recruits to work through an established political party to instigate reform measures and Canyon County Nonpartisans took his advice seriously. In 1918, they took control of the Canyon County Democratic Central Committee and attempted to place their people

Ray McKaig came to Idaho in 1917 and spent several years encouraging farmers to join the Nonpartisan League. (ISHS)

This steam-powered traction engine which worked the ground with discs and harrows, dwarfed the car beside it. (ISHS)

HAYING IN THE 1920s

Today I looked out of my window at the field where one man drove a noisy, monstrous machine that mowed down a wide swath of tall alfalfa, leaving a windrow of fresh mown hay in its wake.

My mind whirled back to the way my father Henry Fujii did it back in the 20's. His team of horses pulled a little two-wheeled mowing machine that had, projecting from one side, a low arm with moving teeth that cut the alfalfa. After the entire field was down, he switched the horses to another machine, a light one with two big wheels, called a rake, with long tines that curved behind like rainbows. He would rake a few yards, then raise the tines, manually of course, repeating until the entire field was in straight windrows. These two steps took oh so many more hours --- days --- in the hot sun than today's one big machine. But I'm sure my mother, watching from her window, marvelled at this labor saving machine that he could ride, remembering the heavy, tall-as-a-man scythe that her father used to wield.

Farmers used horse-drawn mowing machines to cut hay early in the century. (ISHS)

After the hay was in windrows, the team plodded up and down the field the opposite way, raking the rows into a series of little mounds. Then my brother and I joined him in the field with pitch forks to tidy up the mounds into neat piles called shocks. This done, we let the fragrant hay dry a few days.

As do today's farmers.

Ever so often, after weeks on end of dry sunny weather, it rained the rain we'd have welcomed while the alfalfa was growing. My mother used to say the clatter of the mowing machine was the magical signal that invited in the rain clouds waiting behind the mountains. Later, the storm drenched shocks had to dry again, then with pitch forks we turned them over one by one, like heavy fat pancakes, to dry some more.

Today, after the rows of hay are dry --- no need for shocks --- another roaring monster with one man driving, goes down each row devouring the hay in front and ejecting neatly tied bales in back --- in jig time! Later, a group of workers load these onto a huge low trailer and pile them at one end of the field like so many A B C blocks.

Not so, back then!

Haying wasn't just a family affair; it called for neighbors with their team-drawn hayracks and an experienced man to stack. The heavy shocks in the field were pitch-forked high onto hayracks and pulled in to the big red derrick by the barn. From one end of the derrick boom, a Jackson fork with curved tines descended onto a load. It descended because the derrick horse drive --- me --- backed up Belle the big black horse. The man on the hayrack inserted the fork into the hay. At his signal I urged my horse forward, and the fork full of hay lifted, then swung to the man on the haystack. When he'd pushed it to the desired spot he yelled. The man on the hayrack jerked the rope that tripped the fork, dropping the hay. I backed up my horse to bring the fork down for another load. We repeated this process again and again, until the hayrack was empty, and the next waiting load of hay moved in.

So it went, hour after hot, dusty hour, day after day until the huge haystack was expertly formed, shaped like a gigantic loaf of bread, a proper size for the biggest of the big giants in the world.

I started my job as derrick horse driver probably around age 10. I thought this three times a summer job was a nice change from the rows of onions I weeded much of the rest of the summer.

It was a hotter, busier time for my mother, for work crews in those days didn't bring sack lunches or go home at noon. Mama cooked huge platters of meat and potatoes, fried home-raised chicken, vegetables, home-baked bread, pies and cakes, everything from absolute scratch, on the big wood burning stove. Farm wives also prepared mountainous spreads for big threshing crews, potato harvesters, whatever, all before the time of refrigerators, electric ranges and running water. Mama never complained --- it was simply her job, as driving the derrick horse was mine.

The hard, often tedious work didn't hurt us children, not with ambitious, kind, hard-working parents to set an example. We learned the value of having work to do and of getting the job done.

---Mary Henshall

A Jackson fork was used to stack the hay in the early days. (ISHS)

Members of the Hallberg family proudly display their new Case thresher and steam engine. The small tank cart on the left is the water tender for the engine. (CCHS)

into nomination on the Democratic ticket. Statewide, the Nonpartisans failed to take over the leadership positions of the Democratic Party but succeeded in placing their candidates on the ballot as Democrats through heavy participation in the Democratic primary election. Regular Democrats greatly resented this interference with their party.

When election time came in the fall, the Nonpartisans found that they had been overly optimistic regarding their political fortunes. Republicans won a landslide victory in Idaho, defeating all but U.S. Senator John Nugent, a Democrat vying for reelection who was supported by the Nonpartisan League. Following the 1918 general election, the League's opponents cried out for legislation to curb "socialist experimentation" in Idaho. The Republican legislature, with the support of some Democrats,

Two women operate this tractor, shown around 1915. (ISHS)

responded by passing a bill repealing Idaho's direct primary law. This, along with other restrictive measures regulating political parties and elections passed by the legislature, forced the League into a third party status.

In 1920, the Nonpartisans placed candidates on the ballot statewide under the banner of the "Independent Ticket." Farmers claimed Canyon County as a Nonpartisan League stronghold and launched an aggressive campaign, but when the votes were counted the Republicans dominated. The Independent candidate for governor, Sherman D. Fairchild, ran a strong second, however, carrying thirty-three percent of the vote compared with thirty-nine percent of the vote in the county which went to the victor, incumbent Republican Governor D. W. Davis.

The next election year was another story. In 1922, Nonpartisans organized the Idaho Progressive Party and accepted the fact that their candidates were going to have to fight for office from a third party stance. Although the Republican candidate for governor, C. C. Moore, won the election, Canyon County gave him only twenty-nine percent of their vote. They strongly supported H. F. Samuels, the Progressive candidate, with fifty-four percent of the vote in a three-way race.

In county government, the Progressives began a six year reign

Nampa Flour and Feed Company maintained this grain elevator in Nampa early in the century. (ISHS)

that November. They "swept the county, taking every office by pluralities averaging better than two thousand" out of approximately 8500 total votes. The Republican newspaper, the Nampa Leader-Herald, conceded that the Progressives would control the county, but expressed surprise at the size of the Progressive plurality. Knowing that the farming communities would vote "overwhelmingly Progressive," the paper expected the towns to balance out the third party strongholds. However, "Nampa spilled the beans," the paper noted, "giving a more than two to one vote for the Progressives."

In 1924, Republicans maintained control of the statehouse, reelecting Governor C. C. Moore, but Canyon County continued to oppose him, giving H. F. Samuels, the Progressive candidate fifty-six percent of their vote. The Democratic candidate ran an inconsequential race, ending up with only nine percent of the total vote. The county remained staunchly Progressive, with the farmers' candidates retaining their positions in all of the county offices.

Two years later the Republicans were jubilant. They predicted the end of Progressivism in the county and declared that even Canyon County, the "stronghold" of the farmers' third party political movement, "is rapidly revolting against its first complete trial of Progressivism." But their rejoicing was premature. The Progressives continued to control all of the county offices except two, sheriff and county clerk.

By 1928, Republican rule returned to Canyon County government when the Grand Old Party made "a clean sweep" of all the county offices for the first time since 1920. Local candidates rode in on the coattails of Herbert Hoover who took the county by more than a three to one margin in the presidential race. Progressive rule had come to an end.

THE IDAHO FREE PRESS

When the Nonpartisans began their reign in Canyon County, they were suspicious of the local press. The League believed that most of the country's major newspapers were controlled by millionaires who simply published "propaganda sheets." Canyon County newspapers were no exception, said the League. The Nampa Leader-Herald, published by the Jennesses, was, without apologies, a Republican newspaper.   The Nonpartisans found it entirely unsatisfactory because it failed to publish sufficient news concerning the farmers' movements. Needless to say, they also disagreed with its editorial policy. The League also criticized other local newspapers including the Caldwell Tribune, the Boise Statesman and the Boise Capital News.

In 1919, W. G. Scholtz, manager of the Nonpartisan League in Idaho, organized the Cooperative Publishing Company in Nampa. This group, composed largely of farmers, began the first daily newspaper in Nampa, the Idaho Free Press. Calling itself a "people's paper," the Free Press began publication on April 9, 1919, with news items directed to the farming community and an editorial policy strongly sympathetic to the Nonpartisan League.

This well-drilling rig operated near Nampa in the 1920s. (CCHS)

For a three dollar subscription, those looking for an alternative to the town's Republican newspaper could indulge themselves with a paper that crusaded for its favorite causes. Farmers greeted the paper with favor. Within two weeks from the first day of publication, the Idaho State Grange named the Free Press the official Grange paper of Idaho.

With Scholtz as its business manager, the Free Press not only promoted government-sponsored farm programs but also supported the efforts of the working class to form labor unions. In May of 1919, the paper reported with pride that there were over 500 active members of union organizations in Nampa and "the membership is constantly growing. Almost every craft now has its own organization. . ." They found it significant that there was a "growing unity" between "organized farmers and organized labor."

In addition, the newspaper called for the nationalization of the country's natural resources, especially government ownership of the railroads. On April 11, 1919, the Free Press wrote:

> We are in favor of the nationalization of our natural resources, such as mines, waterpowers, fisheries, forests, the means of communication and transportation, and public utilities on which all the people depend.

Highly critical of the profit motives of industrial owners, the paper editorialized, "Not all millionaires are Tories, but most of them are." The paper thought private ownership a "quaint" idea, especially when applied to natural resources.

Scholtz, who started the Free Press, represented the more extreme wing of the Nonpartisan League in Idaho. He was anxious that the organization remain ideologically pure and true to the ideals of Arthur Townley, its founder. Therefore, it was not unusual to find editorials sympathetic to the socialist ideology in the early paper. A week after the first issue was published, the editorial page contained a tribute to Eugene Debs, the Socialist Party leader, who had recently been sentenced to jail.

On May 2, 1919, the paper published an editorial critical of the anti-sedition laws which were in effect across the nation during the World War I era and accused authorities of needlessly limiting free speech. The paper excused those who mailed bombs to prominent citizens nationwide in April of 1919, believing that their actions were caused by repressive measures on the part of the government. "When excitable men are not allowed to talk with their tongues it is an old lesson of experience that they will begin to talk with dynamite," the paper concluded.

This editorial caused a storm of protest in Nampa and the surrounding communities. Concerned citizens organized a meeting at the city hall the afternoon that the editorial appeared. The meeting was attended by twenty-five people. When the editorial in question was read to the group, they began to yell for a bomb to blow up the Free Press building. Ned Jenness, owner of the Free Press's rival, the Nampa Leader-Herald, said, "We must get the Free Press in bad some way [sic]. . . If we can't find a bomb we can get a gas shell. That makes a noise and a stink."

Several groups passed resolutions condemning the Free Press for being un-American and called for the resignation of the paper's editorial staff. The World War Veterans of Canyon County denounced the "grossly inflammatory and Socialistic" articles published by the paper. Those offended by the Free Press articles went so far as to encourage Judge McClear, the federal prosecutor in Boise, to send copies of the paper to the U. S. Attorney General asking for instruction "as to whether or not the sheet shall be barred from the privileges of the mails under the sedition laws." Nothing came from this action, however.

But those who opposed the paper kept the pressure on. They called the paper's organizers socialists and Bolshevics. The paper's reputation spread beyond Nampa as evidenced by an article in the Pocatello Tribune which referred to the town as "the socialist center of Idaho" because of the activities of the Free Press and the Nonpartisan League.

The Free Press had been in existence for a little over a month when a lawsuit was filed against it in May of 1919 by a couple of local citizens who tried to stop the newspaper's publishing company from selling stock. The paper contended that the suit had been filed

In 1923, Nampans tagged their cars, proudly proclaiming that Nampa was the home of the cow, the pig and the hen. (CCHS)

BLACKSMITHING IN NAMPA

Freight teams, headed for Silver City, stand in front of the Star Livery Feed and Sale Stable. (ISHS)

The blacksmith shop of Francis Marion Ruse was located at 1319 First Street South. It is pictured here around 1912. (ISHS)

A. L. Gowen's first blacksmith shop, shown around 1905, was located on the corner of Eleventh Avenue and First Street North. (ISHS)

Gowen built a new $4000 shop in 1909. (ISHS)

A. L. Gowen, left, stands inside his blacksmith shop. (ISHS)

Gowen held the patent on the hay derrick commonly used throughout Idaho. He built approximately a thousand of them in all. (ISHS)

This Nampa business made and sold harnesses. (ISHS)

on mere "technical grounds" by Nampa "malcontents" who simply opposed the efforts of farmers to organize.

When the case went to court, the attorneys for the Free Press, M. H. Eustace and Harry S. Kessler, argued that the plaintiffs were simply "dissatisfied and disgruntled" because they were not elected directors at the annual stockholders meeting. Their real purpose in bringing the suit, said the counsel for the paper, was to interfere with the business, circulation and advertising of the Free Press. The Nampa Leader-Herald admitted that the purpose of the suit was to oust W. G. Scholtz as manager of the paper.

Judge Ed I. Bryan dismissed the action of those suing the Free Press, deciding the civil case in favor of the new paper, but within a week the paper was sued again. This time Ned and Harold Jenness, publishers of the Nampa Leader-Herald, sued the Free Press for libel. This case went to the Idaho Supreme Court where four years after it was initially filed, the high court reversed a lower court jury decision which had awarded the Jennesses one hundred dollars damages plus attorney fees. The Supreme Court found that the evidence was not sufficient to justify a finding of libel.

The Free Press withstood the assaults of those who tried to shut it down in its earlier days, but it also moderated its publishing policies. By July of 1919, the daily column, "Little Lessons in Civics," which was consistently socialistic in ideology, was discontinued. In December of the same year, Scholtz resigned as business manager of the newspaper and was replaced as a member of the board of directors a few months later. Although the annual meeting expressed satisfaction at the showing made by the retiring management, the change signified an effort on the part of the Free Press to enlarge its audience and offend fewer people.

THE FARM DEPRESSION

The farming from the farm taught me patience. A farmer learns to wait. He plants the seed in the spring and harvests in the fall. The farmer has been conditioned to wait. The city man has to have things happen today, now.

---Howard Hartman

While farmers were busy organizing in order to improve their conditions, other factors beyond their control influenced the stability of their occupation. World War I brought on exceptionally high wartime crop prices. Farmers reacted by expanding their farming operations, many buying expensive new ground. Others invested in farm machinery, planning to expand their production. By 1919, many farmers had invested heavily in improvements to their farms, going into debt but hoping to increase their income.

They did not count on what happened next. After the war, the bottom fell out of farm prices, a disaster which brought on a twenty year depression in the agricultural industry. Whereas Idaho corn sold for $1.65 a bushel in 1919, by 1921 the going price was 50 cents. Idaho potatoes went for $1.51 in 1919 but fell to 31 cents in 1922. The economics of the agricultural industry affected the whole Boise Valley which experienced very little growth during the 1920s. In Nampa, the 1910 decade saw an eighty-one percent increase in population during the ten year span, yet from 1921 to 1930, the population of the town increased only 7.6 percent.

Farmers tried to cope by changing the type of crops they raised between 1920 and 1924. Clover hay and alfalfa decreased in acreage, for example, while barley and Indian corn almost doubled in acreage. The number of acres planted in beans nearly quadrupled. But by 1924 the farmers were feeling the agricultural depression and some farmers and tenants began moving away from the area.

While the rest of the country experienced a surge of prosperity prior to the stock market collapse in 1929, farmers felt the improving economic conditions only marginally. Farm prices rose in 1925 and in 1927 the market for crops improved. But farmers suffered along with the rest of the nation during the 1930's depression. Bartering became a common solution for lack of markets for farm goods. However, some crops were left unharvested. By 1932, the value of the farmers' crops had dropped by two-thirds in comparison with two years earlier. In 1933, farmers described their condition as "desperate."

Agricultural land values improved slightly in 1935. The next couple of years again saw a change in farm crops. The Nampa Chamber of Commerce led an effort to secure again a sugar beet factory in the Nampa area and, thus, solicited contracts for over

Pickles were made at the H. J. Heinz plant east of Nampa in the 1920s. Raising top grade cucumbers was tedious work for the farmers and, thus, the plant went out of business after a few years. (CCHS)

Mrs. Fogarty was very, very Irish. She was a short lady, rather chunky. In those days water was scarce. In fact, there were more people killed in the early days over water than there were in gunfights. A mad farmer with a shovel was a lethal weapon. Anyway, on the irrigation water, they had to take turns --- one person would have it for one day, the next person would have it for the next day and so on. Mrs. Fogarty had a little problem getting all of her garden and pastures irrigated in one day. The next day the neighbor went up to see what was going on. The water just wasn't coming through. Mrs. Fogarty was sitting in the ditch. Of course, the water was running out of her outlet. They chastised her about it and she said, "Can't a lady even take a bath?"

--George Jacobsen, Jr.

4000 acres of sugar beets for the 1937 season. It was not until October of 1942 that the Amalgamated Sugar Company began operation of a two million-dollar plant in Nampa, but in 1937 the company had paid the freight costs to encourage Nampa farmers to grow sugar beets. Greater production of sugar beets and truck crops increased the seasonal labor from Mexico in this valley.

By the 1940s the farmers' situation improved considerably. Agricultural prices jumped approximately forty percent between 1940 and 1941. In 1941, the completion of a major highway between southern Idaho and California meant a larger market potential for local farmers. As was the case with the economy in general, agriculture finally established a firm footing again during the years of World War II.

Nampa continues to be dependent upon its agricultural community. In 1970, there were 2395 farms, averaging approximately 131 acres each, in Canyon County. Over eighty-four percent of the land area of the county was farm ground. But the number of people employed in agriculture had decreased. Whereas 5055 people, or approximately forty-five percent, of those employed were engaged in agricultural occupations in 1930, only 3354 people, or approximately fourteen percent, worked in this area in 1970.

Following World War II, farming continued to be a major enterprise in the Nampa area. (Courtesy, Jerry Cornilles)

Hand labor supplemented mechanization in the farm industry in the 1950s. (Courtesy, Jerry Cornilles)

Several food processing businesses, including Birds Eye, located in or near Nampa in the 1940s and 1950s. (Courtesy Jerry Cornilles)

Sugar beets once again became a common crop in the Nampa area after the Amalgamated Sugar Company began operation of its two-million dollar plant in October of 1942. (Courtesy, Jerry Cornilles)

VII
The Depression:
1929 - 1941

Most of the country dates the beginning of the Great Depression from the stock market crash in 1929. In Idaho, however, and in particular in the Nampa area, an agricultural depression began in the early 1920s. It affected business conditions on the whole because the town based its economy in large part on the surrounding farm operations. Nampa's first depression-related bank failure did not happen in the 1930s, but took place in the first half of the 1920 decade.

According to John Brandt, the Nampa State Bank failed in the early 1920s. He recalled, "I was saving money to go to college in the Nampa State Bank, which was in the old Shakey's building. I had saved up probably $400 or $500 and the darn thing went broke and took my money."

When the Nampa State Bank closed in the early 1920s, it was located across the street from the location shown in this picture. Several banks occupied this building on the corner of Twelfth Avenue and First Street South through the years, including the Nampa State Bank and the Bank of Nampa which failed earlier in 1913. (ISHS)

Facing Page: First Street South was known as Main Street when this picture was taken in 1936. (ISHS)

Here are the doors of the Nampa State Bank on the corner of Twelfth Avenue and First Street South. The building was constructed after the 1909 fire. (CCHS)

A couple of years later, a second bank closed. George Jacobsen remembered the impression it made on him as a young person:

> I remember when the Stockman's National Bank went broke in 1924. I had been mowing lawns in the summer time to get enough to buy a bicycle and this bicycle was $24.95. I had been saving a year for it and I knew that Rainbow bicycle was just exactly what I wanted. I had $23.00 in my savings account and I made about a dollar a week mowing different lawns. By golly I'd mowed two weeks and I had my two dollars. That made twenty-five dollars. That morning I went down to the bank to draw my money out and the bank was closed, so I didn't get my bicycle. [In] about six months, they paid out fifty cents on the dollar and then there were a couple of more payments. They paid out.

It took George a year before he bought his bike.

By the 1930s, the entire country acknowledged a general state of economic depression. Again, the agrarian nature of the community influenced the way in which the nationwide depression affected Nampans. Some felt that the Depression was not severe in Nampa. Even though money was scarce, most people had food to eat. Howard Hartman recalled:

> In the Depression, we didn't hardly know it was a Depression. We lived out on a ranch and we had all the eggs and meat and the butter [we wanted.] We butchered a beef, you know, and so on and so forth.

Kern Blakeslee also recollected that it was easier to live on a

Typical of the 1930s is this farm scene taken at the Richard Agenbroad homestead, seven and a half miles south of Nampa on Twelfth Avenue Road. (CCHS)

farm during the Depression. Years later, he remembered:

> Most farmers in the Great Depression, if they
> could scare up enough money to pay their
> taxes and their water bill, then they got along
> pretty well because at that time, everybody
> lived mostly off what they raised. Everybody
> had cows, pigs, [and] chickens. If you had
> wheat you'd take a couple of sacks down to
> the mill here in Nampa and have it ground
> into flour. So of the natives here, even the
> people here in town, there were few who had
> to go hungry.

The Blakeslee family had a small farm, but even that was enough to
generate a little cash flow, according to Kern. His family milked
from five to nine head of cows, bringing in a regular milk check
which often averaged thirty dollars. It was enough money so that
"we were never rich, but we were never destitute."

Howard Hartman also recalled the income generated by milk-
ing cows on the farm:

> My dad got ten cents a gallon for milk. He
> put out a ten gallon can of milk. He got a
> dollar. The time of year when the cows were
> putting out three cans of milk, he got three
> dollars a day. Well, those months he got
> ninety dollars a month, and that was a

But there is no doubt that on the whole money was scarce
during the Depression days. Flossie Stark recalled, "I just thought
that that was the way things were. We didn't have any money and
didn't expect to get any money." Elmo Crill had similar
recollections, but he said lack of money didn't stop the young
people from entertaining themselves. He remembered:

> Nobody had any money. There was no T. V.
> [and] very little radio. You made your own
> entertainment. One of the popular sports of
> everybody at that time was roller skating on
> the sidewalks. [We] would have big parties.

*The Nampa High School band is shown
here in 1933. (Courtesy, Charles
Hanson)*

YORGASON DANCE HALL

"The gathering place was Yorgason Dance Hall that sat on the corner of Eleventh Avenue and Fifth Street North. It was a great big dance hall. When Yorgason built it he built it pretty much on a shoestring and it had walls but it didn't have a roof. He had an orchestra and when you went in you bought tickets for five cents a dance. The orchestra would play a little while and people would move through the crowd to collect the tickets. Then when that dance was finished everybody would go sit down and then they would start another one. After prosperity hit them and they did very well, they finally put a roof on it. Then they could have their dances in the winter time."

---Harry Robb

The Yorgason Dance Hall, located on Eleventh Avenue North, provided hours of entertainment for Nampans during the 1920s and 1930s. (Courtesy, Scott McKnight)

Ernest and Joseph Yorgason who ran the dance hall are shown in the bottom left of this picture. (Courtesy, Scott McKnight)

There would be fifteen people in a group roller skating at one time. Usually we'd end up at somebody's house and have refreshments or go someplace and buy a hamburger for five cents. In those days we didn't miss money because nobody had any.

The younger generation seemed the most immune from the Depression, but although some have memories of the Depression not being severe in this area, others recall extreme hardships. Even though farmers could provide their families with food so that few had to go hungry, the Depression influenced the economic stability of their occupation. Farm prices took a tremendous drop during this period. At times, it was not worth even harvesting the crop. Howard Hartman recalled:

These cars lined up on Twelfth Avenue Road south of Nampa for a farm sale in 1936. (Courtesy, Ruth Allen)

I remember my dad one time had twenty acres of potatoes, and he couldn't even get enough out of them to pay a nickel for the sack. The sacks were a nickel. So he just dug them, and we put an ad in the paper. [We] told the jeweler and the doctors and the businessmen to come out and pick up what they wanted for the winter, one sack for them and one sack for [Dad] to put in a pit and cook up for his hogs.

The thing is, we raised good crops --- that was back in the Thirties, we raised good crops, but we couldn't get any money for them. And so, my dad was depressed about it. My family was depressed about it. Dad only had five thousand dollars on his farm, but he had a hard time paying the five percent, two-hundred and fifty dollars a year to the federal land bank. When things are down like that, and you're raising good crops, you know things were tough.

In town, people also suffered because of the Depression.

This turkey day parade attracted a crowd in downtown Nampa in the 1930s. (CCHS)

Numerous Nampans have memories of scraping by in order to live during these years. For example, Leonard Bowles recalled:

Those were tough days. They talk about the recession now and bad times and, of course, we have 'em, but that Depression was a real honest-to-God depression. People didn't work and when they did work they didn't make very much money.

There were five in our family and at one time my father supported the whole family on thirty dollars a month. That paid the rent, bought the groceries, [and] paid the power bill. Of course, we didn't have a telephone; we didn't have a lot of the luxuries.

I can remember doing everything to get by. We went out and picked up potatoes and beans. They raised lettuce around here at that time, two crops a year and during the lettuce harvest there would be a lot of what they call cull heads. We would gather them. Twice a year we had a lot of salad, but we survived it.

We used to go out and cut sagebrush and bring it in to burn and go down to the railroad yard and the gondolas that they hauled the slack coal in would have a little pile of coal in each corner. We would dump it into a gunnysack and gather that coal to burn.

Times were tough, but families stuck together. Kids all went to school and none of us dropped out. So we have nothing to complain about but it was tough. There is no question about it.

George Jacobsen remembered a family that came into Lloyd Lumber Company where he was working. They had done about everything they could to prepare themselves to survive the winter, but still lacked sufficient fuel for heating their home. This family, according to Jacobsen:

. . .lived on the north side. They were a good family [with] several children. They were ambitious. [The father] came into the store there one evening and told Mr. Lloyd that he'd like to unload a car of coal to get some coal for the real cold weather.

He said, 'I think I'm all set for the year, for the winter, because I worked for one farmer and I took half of my wages in three or four hogs. I took a little cash which was kept to pay our light and water bill. I worked for another farmer and I took grain for my wages so that I could feed the hogs. I've picked up potatoes for another fellow and we've got our potatoes and onions that we need. We've been cutting willows out at the lake for our firewood. My wife and the kids raised a big garden. I think we are just all right for the winter if I can just get some coal in case it really gets bitterly cold.'

That's the way most of us got by.

Coal was the principal fuel used for heating homes. Other

Lloyd Lumber Company supplied coal for the town during the Depression years. (CCHS)

people were not so straightforward about their need for coal, and tried to scrounge what they could when the coal cars came into town on the trains. Again, George Jacobsen recalled:

> When the Depression started, things got pretty tough. I went to work for Lloyd Lumber Company in 1931 and I know that we'd have a shortage on every car of coal that came in from a thousand to two thousand pounds. Nothing much was said about it.
>
> We had the big coal chute right there by the Lloyd Lumber Company, People would come in there every night and they'd pick up any pieces of coal that had fallen on the ground. Why, they took 'em home.
>
> The freight trains would have to slow down almost to a stop out by King's Packing Company. People would hop on those coal cars and start throwing coal off, then they'd go back and pick it up. Well as long as they weren't really going too strong on it not much was said about it. But it wasn't long before one bunch would get on the car and start throwing coal off as the train moved into Nampa. Another bunch would wait until they were out of sight and then they'd come along and pick up the other guys' coal. The good ol' days.

This train derailed east of Nampa in March of 1939. (Courtesy, Carl Martin)

Ben Waigand had recently married about the time the Depression started. He remembered how they got by:

> One thing that did help us a lot and many others too, I think, was the fact that there

The Depression: 1929 - 1941

The Greenleaf Creamery came to Nampa in the 1930s, eventually locating on Second Street South. Shown from left to right are Harold Klefman, Oscar Ax, Oscar's sister, Earl Antrim, owner of the business, and Emmett Herlocker. (Courtesy, Edith Campbell)

were quite a few produce houses in the area. We used to go down to the produce houses and pick up the culls, which were sometimes about as good as the first. Of course, about that time I was just married [and] I didn't have anything.

Also the creameries were operating and we used to go to the creamery with a gallon jug and pick up a gallon of buttermilk or a couple of gallons and we would drink that and also use it to make hotcakes. It made wonderful hotcakes with soda. So with a little flour and a few gallons of buttermilk at a nickel a gallon you had a pretty good meal. And then beans were plentiful. Everybody, well, they just ate accordingly. When you haven't got

The Greenleaf Creamery manufactured ice cream in Nampa from 1930 to December of 1969 when the business was sold. (Courtesy, Edith Campbell)

cake you eat beans. That's the way it went.

People just accepted [the Depression] and figured it was a bad time and maybe it would get better, we hoped. In the meantime, we would just have to do the best we could. So we scrounged and did the best we could.

Ben Anketell thought that the Depression hit the Nampa area pretty hard. He was fortunate enough to find work part of the time during the Depression years, but still life was not easy. He remembered, "I worked for the power company, and in '31 they had the big layoff and cut our line crew from forty-three men down to three." After he was laid off at the power company, he was notified of a job constructing the Salmon Falls dam at Hagerman. Ben bought a 10' x 12' tent and went there with his wife in their Studebaker car. In a little over a month, he made sixty-some dollars. Then, he returned to Nampa:

I bought some lumber and built a tent-frame out here and put the tent on it and the missus and I and our daughter lived in that for a year and a half during the Depression. We got along. And we went out to the lake and cut willows for wood. [We] lived on five bucks a week.

For those who were trying to manage their own businesses, conditions were particularly difficult. At that time, Harold Murray had a box factory in Nampa near Kohlerlawn Cemetery. When the banks started closing, he lost the finances for his business. According to Murray, "The bank conditions so tied us up [that we were] completely stymied for one whole year." Consequently, the business eventually closed. Murray recalled, "The Depression made me start all over again. I had a good start, but the Depression . . ."

Before George Jacobsen went to work for Lloyd Lumber Company, his family lived on very little during the early years of the Depression. He remembered:

There was times when, well, we had one pair of shoes. Many times we would cut heavy cardboard and put in there so the hole wouldn't go through. Somewhere I have a log book that mother kept of the money for the cream check and the eggs. The average income per month then was about twenty-eight dollars, but mother usually had about two dollars of that twenty-eight left.

Fresh meat was a luxury. I had my little twenty-two, a single-gauge four-barrel shotgun, and ducks, pheasants in season or out of season, it didn't make much difference --- that was our fresh meat. We didn't waste anything and we didn't shoot hens. I still don't enjoy eating pheasants.

MAY DAY IN LAKEVIEW PARK

"We would work for weeks constructing these beautiful, beautiful lanterns out of milk cartons or boxes. Then we would march around the bowl at Lakeview Park after the Maypoles had been strung. I thought it was the most beautiful experience to look across [the bowl]. The school children would almost circle the bowl. It was beautiful."

---Margaret Keim Goering

School children dressed in costume and wound the Maypole on the first of May in Lakeview Park. Then a lantern parade followed in the evening. (Courtesy, Mary Henshall and CCHS)

Perhaps the hardship of the Depression made itself felt the most during the Christmas season. At least such was the case with the Jacobsen family. Jacobsen looked back at those years:

The Ambrose Johnson family enjoys a picnic in the park in the late 1920s. (Courtesy, Sumner Johnson)

I remember Christmas in 1930. That was probably the low point in our family. You could buy a nice Christmas tree for a quarter but we didn't have the quarter. So I went up in the sagebrush and I got a nice sagebrush and brought it home and put a stand under it. We popped corn. Mother had some cake coloring, so we decorated that popcorn [and] decorated the tree. Of all the Christmas trees we've had I remember that Christmas tree more than any we ever had.

But that 1930 Christmas --- I remember I had a $2.50 gold piece that my grandad had given me and mother asked me if she could have the $2.50 gold piece because we were absolutely stranded. Why sure she could. I remember she and dad sitting down there just figuring out what they could buy with the $2.50 that would go the fartherest. This was groceries. No foolishness, that was flour and ---

Oh we ground our own flour. [I remember] good ol' whole wheat bread. You know there is nothing in the world that is as good as homemade bread. Mother always baked on Friday. I knew when I'd get home from school that there was that hot bread just out of the oven. Just cut a slice about three inches thick off the end of one of those loaves, put homemade butter on top of it and you could see it melt down into the bread. Get a glass of buttermilk, you know, [with] flakes of butter floating around in it. That was living!

The things that meant so much were the simple things.

Sumner Johnson also had childhood memories of Christmas during the Depression. In 1933, he remembered, his folks had absolutely no money. But they managed to find a Christmas present for their boys. According to Sumner:

> Apparently the day before Christmas the folks went to Boise and they found a broken toy that was a little steam engine type thing. It was round at the base, maybe about three inches in diameter, and came up as a cylinder. On the top it had a flywheel and it had a little petcock that you could turn so that when steam was generated steam would come out there and make a whistling effect. Down at the base, inside that cylinder, was a little place to put a kerosene lamp burner thing in it.

> Anyway, that flywheel had been broken and dad figured out that he could weld it. They bought it, at a very great discount because it was broken, and brought it home and that night welded or soldered the thing back together.

> That was the one toy for us three boys on Christmas morning. I was only eight or nine years old and my mother was scared to death of me using it but Wayne, my older brother, would actually light the matches, get the burner going, put the water in, and then that flywheel would get to going and we'd open that petcock and the thing would whistle.

> Greatest toy I ever had in my life, and that was the sole toy for the three of us there that Christmas --- a far cry from now-a-days. So that was just kind of an indication of what you did.

The bottom fell out of prices on most items in this area. Ed Ware remembered that he could buy milk for seven cents a quart, eggs for approximately ten cents a dozen, and peaches or pears for a dollar and a quarter a bushel. Elmer Burri priced a whole beef at five dollars and a hog at two dollars and fifty cents. Leonard Bowles confirmed those memories:

> I remember hamburger was seven cents a pound and eggs were five or ten cents a dozen, something like that. A pound loaf of bread was a nickel. You could go to the grocery store and have a hard time carrying out ten dollars worth of groceries. You

didn't make much money but you didn't have to spend too much money either, but it was tough.

Willis and Frances Coyle were married during the Depression in 1934. (Courtesy, Frances Coyle)

Willis and Frances Coyle were married during the Depression in 1934. Willis was fortunate to have a job at the Pacific Fruit Express shop, but Frances kept careful track of how they spent their money. Looking at her log years later, she discovered:

> We bought a half a ton of coal and wood for five dollars and sixty cents. We bought flour and lard for a dollar twenty-three. I bought an awful lot of flour and lard, so I must have fried in it all the time.
>
> To my brother, Guy, I must have borrowed a dollar for a dress, because I paid it back, a dollar. We bought my sister a pair of shoes for a dollar. Our lights were two dollars and twenty-five cents. I think we lived on flour and lard, and milk and eggs that we bought

from my mother. Our rent was eight dollars a month.

We bought Willis overalls for a dollar or a dollar and a half. He got paid twice a month. The first part was thirty dollars and fifty-three cents and the second half was twenty-eight dollars and sixty-one cents. So, that made a little over fifty-nine dollars a month for wages.

For those who did not have cash, a lot of bartering took place. For example, Dr. Thomas Mangum took produce or meat in exchange for medical services. His son, Dr. Bob Mangum, recalled:

During those years, much of Dad's income came from produce. Farmers would bring in half a beef or half a pig or something like that and they would put it in the freezer. And then we lived on produce a lot. I also remember during those years that Dad had to pay income tax on all his produce and it was a pretty tough sledding.

Not everyone would barter, however. Mrs. Effie Isgrigg remembered trying unsuccessfully to exchange wood for soap:

I'd run pretty low on groceries and I needed soap so badly, so I went over to the store --- clear downtown. The stores were not like these supermarkets at all, where you go and help yourself. The man would come to meet you with a big smile on his face and [say], "What will you have today?"

I said, "Well, I, I need some soap and some other things but I don't have any money. Could I exchange wood for some soap?"

He just froze. He said, "No, indeed not!" He turned coldly away and that was it. So I started home, kind of dreary like, you know, moping along 'til I got clear out to our place on 119 Juniper.

As I walked home that night it seemed like a cold, cold world ---a cold cruel world. For the first time in my life I felt the coldness when you don't have any money in your pocket --- not a dime.

The Depression generated a spirit of cooperation among some people in the town. One Nampa businessman said that he had never seen such demonstrations of friendship and acts of compassion as those extended to fellow human beings during the days of the Depression. Leonard Bowles also remembered the sense of community that existed in the business sector of the town:

The Nampa D, also known as Falk's Department Store, occupied the building at the corner of First Street and Thirteenth Avenue South in 1936. (ISHS)

In those days you depended on other people. If one of the guys downtown with a business got in trouble then the rest of the guys in downtown business would rally around him and give him a boost and help him out. They done that for one another and that is why and how they got through it.

Much business was transacted on credit, according to Elmo Crill. Charge accounts were common, especially at the grocery stores. Consequently, when a bank closed and currency was scarce, merchants allowed goods to be sold without an exchange of money. During the bank holiday in March of 1933, the Nampa Department Store opened twenty-five new accounts in one day in order to accommodate people without cash.

During one bank closure, which was caused by a "run" on the bank, local businessmen joined together to organize a system to protect the bank's deposits. The businessmen prepared waivers which they took to people who had a bank balance of more than $200. The depositors who signed the waivers agreed voluntarily to limit their withdrawals from the bank over a period of two years. The procedure allowed the bank to reopen with the depositors receiving interest-bearing certificates for the amounts of their deposits which were frozen.

When President Roosevelt declared a bank holiday in March of 1933, closing all of the nation's banks, the Nampa Chamber of Commerce issued script or "emergency certificates" in denominations of twenty-five cents, fifty cents, one dollar and five dollars. An office, established in the Meffan-Rising real estate building, was staffed by representatives of Nampa's two banks. Those who showed proof of bank balances could receive script equal to ten percent of the amount they held in their checking accounts. Nampa stores, in turn, honored the script as payment for goods and the local utility companies announced that they would accept script as payment for power and light bills, telephone bills and water bills.

Nampa's two banks, the Nampa State Bank and the First Security Bank, were closed for eleven days. When the bank holiday ended, Nampa merchants redeemed more than $6000 worth of script which had been put into circulation during the emergency and the Idaho Free Press, announced that Nampa banks were "deluged with new deposits" and that "there were practically no withdrawals."

Two organizations in town administered charitable relief programs for those who were in need of help. Kern Blakeslee remembered the work of the Salvation Army:

> The Salvation Army did a lot of work here in town in that period. I can well remember, I don't know what year it was, the Salvation Army came out soliciting things and we didn't have any money, but we had apples, lots of them. And our next door neighbor had a cellar full of potatoes and we offered [them] as much as they wanted. They came out with a truck and loaded it up.

Also, the town organized a Community Relief Committee comprised of the mayor, the Salvation Army captain and a citizen member. George Jacobsen remembered that "the first winter when things were pretty bad they got a bunch of flour, a bunch of beans, a bunch of salt pork, [and] enough money together to help people pay their water bill and their light bill." This group also worked with state and federal government officials to coordinate relief efforts.

Some people were fortunate to be able to maintain jobs during the Depression, but even for those who worked, wages were low. Howard Hartman remembered his first job after graduating from Nampa High School in 1932:

Several well-known Nampa men joined Jacob Lockman in celebration of his eightieth birthday in 1937. Included in the picture are, top row, from left: W. C. Adams, Clark Murphy, Tilden Lockman, Jack Lewis and Vic Elver. Seated around the table are, from left: Bob Davis, C. Harvey Moore, E. S. Hamaker, Ned Jenness, Pat Murphy, Jacob Lockman, Ed Hillier, Con Dewey, Dr. George Kellogg and Bill Dinzel, the brewmaster. (CCHS)

The Jake Torch Drug Store was located on Main Street between Eleventh Avenue and Twelfth Avenue South. (CCHS)

I couldn't afford to go to college the first year, so I took a janitor job out at Lone Star School. [It] paid me a dollar a day and I swept out the four school rooms and kept the furnaces going and took care of all the athletics on the playground for a dollar a day.

The experience was not disagreeable to him, however, and when he graduated from the College of Idaho, Hartman went into teaching.

Ben Waigand worked as an electrician when he could find work during the Depression, but he found it difficult to collect on work that he did. He remembered one incident in particular:

I remember wiring one house for an old fellow and most of it was my material cost. Labor wasn't very heavy. I went very cheap on the labor because I wanted to get the job. Then after I got done he didn't pay me and here I was without any material and no money. So I went to him and told him, 'You either pay for it or I am going to take the wire back out of there so that I can put it in somebody else's place.'

I wasn't going to talk to the law about it either. I was just going to do it. He didn't have any money. 'I'll pay you later,' he said. So I went over there and took my stepladder and went up and started to take the wire out of the house and the old guy came over and climbed up the stepladder and yelled at me. He said, 'If you'll stop, I'll give you the money.' He found some money. He paid me. That's the way it was. Conditions were very bad.

Seasonal employment was generally available in the Nampa area during the summer months on the area's farms. Elmo Crill remembered:

> Of course the farms were practically all hand labored. You could always use a fine workman. The haying took quite a crew because it was all put up by hand. Topping of the corn was all done by hand. The beets --- sugar beets --- were all plowed. They just plowed them out of the ground and then you had to go along and cut the tops off. That was a lot of farm labor. You could usually always find some kind of employment on the farm.

But farm wages were particularly low. Leonard Bowles worked in the hay harvest for a dollar a day plus his noon meal. He worked ten-hour days, making an average of ten cents an hour.

When Kern Blakeslee wanted to make a little extra money, he picked prunes. He related the experience:

Sherman and Edith Clark started the Clark Orchard south of Nampa in the 1930s. Their grandson Stephen Clark poses with his other grandfather, Lee Moore, in the orchard in the late 1940s. (Courtesy, Stephen Clark)

This was in 1933 because it was the year of the bank holiday. We got paid six cents a lug for prunes. A lug is a little more than a bushel. It's hard work to pick a bushel of prunes. We worked at that for about a week and I averaged $2.40 a day. A friend of mine that was with me worked a little faster or harder than I and he made about $3.00 a day and we thought that we were getting pretty well paid.

When we got done and the orchard was all picked, we couldn't get our money because the people didn't have any money. We had to go back a couple of weeks later when they had gotten paid for the prunes and they could get some cash. But they couldn't go to the bank and borrow the money. The banks weren't open.

Ed Ware remembered hiring secretarial help during the Depression. Whereas a woman might have made sixty-five dollars a month before the Depression, during the thirties, salaries dropped drastically. "After the Depression came, just average office help --- typing and filing --- women or girls were happy to work for thirty dollars a month here in Nampa in my office," according to Ed.

After the nation elected Franklin Roosevelt president in 1932, the federal government initiated a jobs program as part of the nationwide relief effort. Called the Works Project Administration, or WPA, this project had a two-fold impact on Nampa. It not only helped put Nampans to work, but it allowed the city to make several needed civic improvements. The WPA undertook numerous projects in Nampa, including street improvements and curbing and sidewalk construction. For example, in 1935, Second Street South was widened from Eleventh Avenue to Fourteenth Avenue with labor paid for through a $7992 federal WPA grant.

KFXD started at Jerome, Idaho, broadcasting from a corner of an electrial and radio store in 1924. Henry H. Fletcher is at the receiver in the picture and Frank E. Hurt, owner and operator of the station, is at the mike. (ISHS)

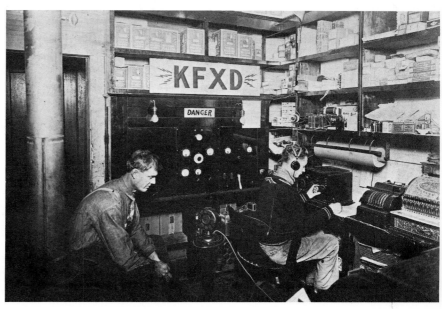

KFXD built its main studio, transmitter and general offices at Nampa in 1930. Here Les Gray, Pete Schmidt, Vera Harris and Walt Harris, known as the Idaho Wranglers, provide music for the listeners of KFXD. (ISHS)

The WPA was instrumental in making needed improvements in Nampa's public schools in the 1930s. In October of 1935, the Idaho Free Press reported that facilities were grossly inadequate for Nampa's school population. Lakeview School averaged thirty-seven students per classroom, whereas Roosevelt's two hundred pupils were housed in six wooden bungalows. The hallways at Kenwood School had been partitioned into rooms in order to provide additional space for the school's 600 students. At the junior high school, classrooms averaged more than forty pupils each and the senior high school recorded an enrollment of 760 in a building meant to hold no more than 400 people.

On October 21, 1935, Nampa property taxpayers approved an $80,000 school bond issue for construction to be done in conjunction with the WPA. Because Nampa passed the bond issue, the city qualified for a WPA allotment of $65,000. Beginning with this funding, Nampa worked with the WPA to make major improvements in its school facilities in the next couple of years.

The WPA made additions or improvements which increased the number of classrooms at Lakeview, Kenwood and the senior high schools. They put up a six-room structure at Eastside School, replacing bungalow and basement classrooms. Workers built a gymnasium at the senior high school and an auditorium with a seating capacity of 2200 at the junior high school. The six bungalows at Roosevelt School were replaced with a twelve-room brick school building. In the late 1930s, President Roosevelt visited Nampa, greeted the people and acknowledged the work that had been accomplished in town during his administration.

In addition to the WPA, Nampans also found jobs through the New Deal's Civilian Conservation Corps program. Most of the CCC work was done in Idaho forests; however, there was a CCC camp at Lake Lowell that helped with maintenance of the dams and the federal game reserve.

Several Nampans remembered working for the WPA or the CCC. For example, one day when Willis Coyle was searching for a job he saw a long line at the city hall. He recalled his experience:

President Franklin D. Roosevelt toured the Boise Valley, visiting Nampa in September of 1937. He greeted the people of the town and acknowledged Roosevelt grade school which was named after him. (Courtesy, Ruth Allen)

I don't know what you call the New Deal, but, I'll tell you, [it was] a New Deal for me. I was downtown one time, looking for a job, and I met two or three of my buddies. We walked around that one day and noticed that line of --- clear to the city hall --- of men. So we walked up and asked what was the line-up for. 'Oh, we're applying for a job.' So, we were all looking for a job, so we just stood in line. And that's how I got in the three C's.

[The interviewer] said, 'Did you ever drive a truck?' I said, 'Yes.' And I had never drove a truck in my life. So he said, 'You stand right over there, with them other guys over there.' So that's how I got to become a truck driver for the government. I spent twelve months with them. . . . It was the beginning of a new era.

Lloyd Castagneto worked as a supervisor for the WPA and was involved, in particular, with the construction of Roosevelt School. He remembered the pride the men took in their work:

Most of those fellows were men who had families and they wanted to work hard and do a good job. They wanted something to show for what they had done when it was all over. They took a lot of pride in the schools because they knew their kids were going to go to school there and such.

During the Depression, there was a certain group of people who, unable to find steady work, travelled across the country in

NAMPA POST OFFICE

The Nampa Post Office, shown here in the early 1950s, was built on the corner of Eleventh Avenue and Second Street South in 1930. (Courtesy, Elaine Chapin)

The post office is pictured in the early stages of construction in August of 1930. (CCHS)

The interior of the new post office is photographed before the building was completely finished. (CCHS)

search of jobs and food. Commonly referred to as "hobos," these people were generally treated with dignity by Nampans, although they were separated as a group unto themselves and were not generally considered a part of the community.

Nampa had an abundance of transients because of being on the main line of the railroad. One railroad worker estimated that on a local freight train that came out of Pocatello six days a week, as many as one hundred riders hopped the thirty-car train. The railroad management didn't simply ignore those who were "riding the rails," but because of the numbers of people involved, they had very little control over the situation. A few of the transients were inconsiderate and would do such things as build a fire on a wooden platform, according to Kern Blakeslee who worked for the railroad during these years. Most of them wouldn't bother anybody.

In Nampa, the transients congregated in an area known as "Hooverville" or "Hobo Junction." Ben Waigand said you could see their fires at night where they were cooking their dinners in tin cans. Bill Castegneto described this area:

> Just to the North of us was the PFE Ice Plant and the railroad tracks. Close by were what was known then as the Hobo Junction which was occupied by lots of hobos coming through the area riding the rails.
>
> Because we were so close to them, I remember very vividly that we had quite a large contingent of so-called hobos in town at all times and for some reason they frequented our back door probably as much as anybody in town, always knowing that there was a handout from my mother. All of them were willing to do a little work for what they got, spading the garden or doing a little trimming or touch-up around the house.
>
> We were instructed that although they seemed to be nice people, [we were] never to go down to the Hobo Junction, but we, like all kids, were filled with a lot of inquisitiveness and we would venture down there.

Several Nampans recalled the steady stream of "hobos" that came through town during the Depression. Most were willing to trade work for food. Kern Blakeslee remembered:

> Mostly they were just looking for work of some sort and it got down to where a man would practically go door to door looking for work, any kind of work.
>
> One summer on the threshing crew we had, oh, three or four transient laborers, bums, hobos, as we called them at that time. I remember particularly one. He was a real good worker; he pitched bundles out in the

field, kept up with everyone else. When the day was over, most people would run down to the canal to clean up. They'd strip off their clothes and when he did he took off one of his legs. He had an artificial leg and he'd worked out there in the field all day, a ten hour day, and kept up with everybody. It was noticed that he limped a little, but not seriously.

The "hobos" went door-to-door in the community asking for hand-outs. Harry Robb recalled:

In a community like this, as small as it was, it was not uncommon to have somebody knocking on your door begging. They would want to know if you had any work they could do for something to eat. They rode the freight trains, traveling in both directions looking for work. That's what the depression amounted to, an awful lot of going back and forth.

The Richard Keim family posed for this picture at a family picnic in the 1930s. (Courtesy, Margaret Keim Goering)

The Nampa City Band provided entertainment for the community. This photo was taken in May of 1938. (Courtesy, Carl Martin)

I don't remember anyone being turned away from my home. My mother would rustle something up, a sandwich or something for them to eat. There was nothing more sad than a man that was hungry with no place else to go.

Margaret Keim Goering also remembered that her family treated the transients with sympathy when they came to their home in search of food. She recalled:

We lived right next to the tracks because we lived at the H. H. Keim Meat Packing Plant and there wasn't a day that went by that someone didn't come up the tracks and ask for food or a job or something.

I don't know of a single time that my folks turned anyone away. Quite often Dad would give them a small job, something to do to pay for their food, but they never turned them away. I have thought of that so many times because we had gardens and we would have meat albeit sometimes green because it was what someone didn't buy, but we always had food on the table.

Many of the residents of the town also remembered that the "hobos" had a system of marking houses where residents provided free hand-outs. Ben Waigand said that "they would put a little X on your door or around there someplace, so that the next guy would know that it was a good place to get a handout." The system of designating houses was recognized by other transients, but was not recognizable by the residents of the community.

This is the story of the Depression as told by Nampans who lived in the community in the 1930s. Their experiences vary. Some knew the hardships and tribulations of the time period to a greater degree than others. However, all were influenced by the fact that economic stability did not completely return to the town until the nation became embroiled in World War II.

VIII
World War II and Its Aftermath:
1941 - 1959

The nation struggled to keep out of the conflict which was raging in Europe in the latter part of the 1930s. Idaho's own Senator William Borah was in the forefront of those who held to an isolationist sentiment, staunchly opposing any United States involvement in the war across the ocean. However, by 1941, after the Japanese bombed Pearl Harbor, the American people rallied behind President Franklin Roosevelt and the Congress when they declared war on Germany and Japan. In contrast to World War I, once the United States entered this conflict, there was very little opposition to the war effort.

Many Nampans remember where they were when they heard the shocking news that the Japanese had attacked Pearl Harbor. For example, Marguerite Brown recalled:

> World War II broke out in early December in 1941 when I was a senior in high school. Those of us who were on the "Growl" staff thought we were a rather favored group under the journalism teacher. I can remember sitting around the "Growl" staff office, listening to the President's radio address to the country. December 7 was on a Sunday and this would have been the next day which was a Monday, a school day.
>
> Things began to change very swiftly in high school at that point. The fellas in my graduating class, many of them, were starting to make plans to take some sort of military training or enlist or whatever.

Nampa participated with the rest of the nation in the measures that the war necessitated. Frieda Shaw remembered that "it was just amazing how people cooperated and how they would realize the

Marguerite Spencer Brown, shown here in 1943, remembered being in Nampa when the United States entered World War II. In later years, Brown served on the Nampa City Council from 1975 to 1983. (Courtesy, Marguerite Brown)

Facing Page: The Nampa Greyhound bus depot is pictured in the early 1950s. (Courtesy, Elaine Chapin)

Local residents used ration coupons to purchase many items which were in short supply during World War II. (CCHS)

things that had to be done."

Many items were rationed and required stamps in order to purchase them. Ed Ware remembered volunteering for the ration board, one of approximately fifteen people in Nampa who served in that capacity. To buy sugar, meat, shoes, gas and tires, for example, one had to have ration coupons. Other things were simply hard to get, such as clothespins, soap, hosiery and cigarettes. Bill and Frieda Shaw recalled living with the ration system:

> Shoes. We had to have ration stamps to buy shoes. But gas was the big problem. Gas was rationed, sugar was rationed, and soap was hard to get. Clothespins you couldn't buy any place. They weren't rationed, but ---

> Tires were hard to come by. Almost impossible. They lowered the speed limit to thirty miles an hour, or thirty-five miles. You weren't to drive faster than thirty-five in order to save tires and gasoline. And people cooperated. It was a matter of survival. People seemed to have sense enough to know that.

I was always fortunate because people would give me stamps so I could buy some new shoes. Stockings were hard to get. Just before the war they started making nylon hose and I can remember how wonderful we thought that was, nylon hose. But, of course, there was no such thing as nylon hose then after the war. All the nylon went into parachutes. The nylon was taken for military needs and so we had rayon. But even then, they were very hard to get.

There was a little lady that lived on Sixteenth Avenue across from the Catholic School and she would repair runners in hose. I'd take my hose to her to repair and she would reknit them. She had some kind of a little tool that she used. Can you imagine? I think that she would do that for twenty or twenty-five cents a runner. Now you just throw your hose away when they have runners in them. Anyway, I do.

After graduating from Nampa High School, Marguerite Brown went to Northwest Nazarene College. The ration system affected life at college, but there were ways around it. Brown recalled:

I think it's perfectly fair to say that really truly there was a desperate shortage of men on campus. The only ones that were there were either 4-F's or ministerial students who were deferred. The ministerial students often had something going for them because gasoline and tires were both being rationed.

There weren't that many cars running around at that time, but many of these [ministerial students] had fathers who were ministers who could get tires and didn't have quite the problem getting gasoline so that we could go over to Boise which was a big neat thing to do --- twenty miles away on the old winding Highway 30 --- and we could do some driving around that a lot of other people weren't doing at the time because of that.

George Jacobsen also remembered how they lived with the rationing system. He said:

Rationing. Gas rationing. We got along very well with it; we cooperated pretty well. Of course we all had farm friends and they had unlimited gasoline. Really the gasoline rationing was to conserve tires, not to conserve petroleum. So we'd go out on Sundays. We'd work at the farms. We'd always have a pretty near dry gas tank when we got out there and we'd work all day and come home with some meat and a full gas tank. We got along all right; nobody really abused it.

As I remember a class A ticket only gave you three gallons of gasoline a week. I didn't buy a tire for four years. We never wore one out. Speed limits were very low; everybody was careful. Shoes. The toughest thing on the shoes was the little kids that grew so fast. Meat really wasn't a problem because, as I said, we all had friends on the farms.

Jinx Falkenburg, far right, a well-known actress in the 1940s, visited Nampa to promote the first Nampa Bond Drive during World War II. (CCHS)

Nampa also participated in the blackouts which were practiced as a war-time measure. Elmo Crill remembered:

Of course you had the blackouts. Everything was turned off all the time. Folks was to have the windows shut. They had block wardens that walked around and if they could see a light through the windows then they would knock on your door and tell you to turn the light out.

Jacobsen recalled the first blackout in Nampa, the night of December 21, 1941:

Our third daughter, Linda, was born the night of our first blackout, December 21, 1941. I was a busy guy that night 'cause I was in charge of the auxiliary firemen. My wife, I had just taken her to the hospital. They'd called an alert, so I left her out there to take care of herself.

The first blackout --- of course, we all knew ahead that it was going to be called sometime that night. There was only one nightlight left on in town that shouldn't have been. And [there was] that kind of mob hysteria. 'Let's break out the window and put out that light!' Well that was unnecessary and, of course, we didn't do it.

Many of the young men in Nampa left to fight the war. Consequently, labor was in short supply, especially for the area's farmers. John Brandt remembered having very little help on his farm. "All there was left here to work were 4F's and floaters," Brandt said, and "at one time I operated 190 acres --- that doesn't sound like much now but it did then --- with 4F's and floaters." The army had rejected those classified as 4F's because of physical incapabilities of one sort or another. Floaters were "transients that they couldn't catch up with," according to Brandt.

When the War Department established two German prisoner of war camps in this area, the soldiers occupying the camps helped produce and harvest the area's crops. One camp was located on John Brandt's property in the Franklin district north of Nampa. The second was on the Joe M. Swartz I farm south of town. Censorship prevented the activities of the camps from being widely known in the area.

There were approximately one hundred men housed in the Franklin Camp, according to Brandt. The German POWs kept their military regime and were disciplined by their own officers, although

Bill Schwartz from Nampa served in the Army during World War II. (Courtesy, Ruth Allen)

The four Hanson brothers, Robert, Bruce, Charles and Richard, all left Nampa to spend time in the Navy or the Army during the second World War. (Courtesy, Charles Hanson)

John Brandt remembers using German prisoners of war to operate his farm during World War II. (Courtesy, Idaho Press Tribune)

This tower still stands on the Swartz farm south of Nampa, reminiscent of the days of World War II when a German P.O.W. camp was located on the property. (Courtesy, Idaho Press Tribune)

American armed guards oversaw the camp. An armed guard escorted the POWs to the farms to work, but no one attempted to escape, said Brandt. The Franklin camp operated for about two years.

Brandt remembered how he established some rapport with the Germans:

> Although I was very much adverse to tobacco, they said that if I wanted to keep in good with these guys I should bring them out a can of tobacco. So, I bought the first and only one I ever bought to take out to them. They were very grateful.

Overall, Brandt found the POWs to be very courteous and pleasant. Although they couldn't speak English, Brandt sensed that "they were glad to be prisoners."

Some of the POWs worked for Leonard Tiegs, helping him pick peas, onions and potatoes. Tiegs found the POWs to be excellent help and easy to work with. Although they were working as farm laborers here, in their home country they represented a variety of trades and professions, such as lawyers, steel workers, shoemakers, and watchmakers, in addition to farmers.

Tiegs felt that the prisoners were treated well during their stay here. Although the camps had their own cooks, Tiegs' wife sent sweet rolls, milk and coffee out to them in the fields on occasion. But the local residents were advised not to fraternize with the POWs, according to Tiegs. Women, in particular, were told to stay away from the prisoners.

The POW camp on the Swartz farm south of Nampa was located away from the road in an isolated spot. Built by local farmers, the buildings were made of composition board and had tent roofs. Two guard towers overlooked the complex which housed approximately 250 prisoners. The camp operated for about three years.

Vera Swartz, daughter-in-law of Joe Swartz, remembered when the POWs arrived at the camp:

> We were all curious, so a lot of us stood by the side of the road to see what they were like. They were marched single file all the way to the camp. Some were on crutches and some had arms in slings and were sort of a 'mis-happen' looking bunch of young men. But they all seemed to have recovered.
>
> I was just a young bride at the time and I was scared to death of them. I tried to avoid them as much as possible. I had a lot of mixed feelings about the prisoners. I had many classmates and dear friends who were in the service. We had nothing to do with them other than having them work in the fields.

Flossie Stark's father was the field man for the POWs on the Swartz farm. She recalled visiting with the Germans and having lunch with them and came away thinking that they were so much different than what people thought. "Most of them were actually in the army because they were drafted and they weren't really Nazis," said Stark. "They had some hard core Nazis down there and they kept them segregated. But most of the prisoners that were there were happy to be working in the fields and they sang all the time they were working." Helen Swartz remembered that their favorite song was "Don't Fence Me In."

When the war was over the camps were quickly dismantled and the prisoners, glad to be going home, were returned to Germany. Several area residents received letters from them after they were back in their homeland. A guard tower still stands south of Nampa on the Swartz farm as a reminder of the World War II era.

Mary Fujii Henshall remembers when, as a high school student, she was not welcome at the Nampa public swimming pool because of her race. (Courtesy, Mary Fujii Henshall)

For Japanese-Americans, World War II was a difficult time. Those who lived on the coast were moved inland to internment camps. Those who lived in the Nampa area were not moved, but experienced suspicion and discrimination because of their race.

Mary Fujii Henshall moved to Nampa with her family in 1918, when she was not quite two years old. Her story encompasses more than the World War II era, but gives a feel for what it was like to grow up as a part of a minority race in this area. She recalled:

> I don't remember when I realized I was of a different race, for my parents outside of speaking Japanese at home were quite as American as apple pie and instilled in us the importance of being good American citizens. Perhaps it was the language that made me aware we were different. I learned English mighty fast while learning to read.

> We went to the Southside Methodist Church, truly the little brown church in the wildwood, where my father was treasurer and on the Board of Trustees. I remember the row of rocking chairs at the back where we watched the old men like my father, Albert Lee, and Mr. Fike rock, often dozing while W. W. Deal preached loud enough for the rockers to hear --- no P. A. system in those days. These old men were in their 30s and 40s. Hattie Dye was my loving Sunday School teacher. The Deal children often played their musical instruments: Edson, later Idaho's Secretary of State, violin; Homer, real estate agent, trumpet; Leland, long time educator, trombone. We were totally welcome as the only Japanese family in the church and we loved it.

> My parents shielded us from any prejudice and never spoke of it. For example, they wanted us to learn to swim but did not take us to the local pool. No matter how pressing the farm work, we took many trips to Givens, the pool at Sweet, and even to Starkey Hot Springs. Later when I was in my teens I learned why when I drove in to enroll in the Red Cross life-saving class at the City Pool. I did not understand when the man said, 'We can't allow you in the pool.'

> I still feel the terrible hurt when I realized what the man meant. My father had let me try, thinking I might be accepted. Now, he went immediately to talk to the mayor and the next day I was in the life-saving class --- an unheard of exception had been made. I wish

I knew who the kind mayor was.

When my high school class of '34 had our senior sneak day in Boise I knew by then that I would not be allowed in the Boise natatorium. But in the crush of 200 students, somehow I got in and had a good swim, the only Japanese-American who ever contaminated their water.

There were many instances of prejudice. For example, when a potato growers association was organized here, my father and [Henry] Hashitani went to a meeting to learn how to raise potatoes. No sooner had they entered when they were asked to wait outdoors. A few minutes later a man came out and told them they had just passed a resolution not to allow Japanese in the membership. We are not called the "Quiet Americans" for nothing, for the two Henrys simply nodded their heads and went home. They succeeded in raising excellent potatoes anyway.

I graduated from Nampa High in 1934 where I was the only Japanese-American in my class, in the whole school, in fact. I was totally accepted, very active with offices, even president in clubs as well as class treasurer and class secretary. I went to Oregon State and upon graduation learned that even we who were honor students in law, engineering, education, whatever, could find no jobs better than farm work, house work, or a fruit stand.

Then came World War II.

The government did not put us into concentration camps like the West Coast Japanese, but life was severely restricted and the FBI kept us under constant surveillance. I could not believe that we who were loyal American citizens could be treated as if we were the enemy.

One night some people blasted out the windows of my little house with shot guns. Luckily my year-old baby was directly under a window and I was across the room, so we were not injured though showered with glass. White-hooded people burned a cross in my parents' front yard. My teen-age brother was accused of sending messages to Tokyo and his home-built ham radio equipment was confiscated, as were articles like guns and cameras. For years we hardly went anywhere except to buy food. We were allowed an all Japanese church service in Caldwell. The hill by Twelfth Avenue and Ruth Lane, three-fourths mile from home, had a big sign: NO JAPS WELCOME HERE. All this, while our sons and brothers and husbands were serving in Uncle Sam's army, winning purple hearts. A family in Emmett lost both of their sons.

My father in his quiet way, never bitter, never angry, did not cease his efforts to minimize misconceptions and to work for better understanding. War turns reason to hatred, but the friends and neighbors who knew us were kind, accepting and faithful always. How we appreciated them!

We endured those years not without fear and tears. But the war ended and in time people stopped looking at us as if we were the enemy who dropped the bombs on Pearl Harbor. After all, we of the younger generation were born here and Japan was a foreign country.

My generation, called the nisei (ne-say), were children or very young during the war. Now as young adults, without protest or demonstration, we quietly worked through our country's legislative process and, though

Mary Fujii Henshall taught at Sunnyridge School in 1947 when this picture was taken. (Courtesy, Mary Fujii Henshall)

Cultural boundaries are bridged by these Japanese children. To help celebrate the Nampa Harvest Festival, the children dressed in traditional Japanese costumes and rode on a Japanese float but they waved American flags, demonstrating their loyalty to the United States, the country in which they were born. (Courtesy, Mary Henshall)

it took a few years, succeeded in having the anti-land laws and others repealed. We won citizenship rights for our parents and even were allowed to marry Caucasians.

I feel so totally American that I forget my ancestry. Until a stranger asks me where I came from; or a good friend says in all sincerity, 'I like the Japanese'; or until I learn that my grandson, a fourth generation American, was classed as an Asian, along with recently arrived Vietnamese immigrants, and refused admission to a racially balanced school in Southern California.

Then I look in a mirror and laugh, for I do look like my cousins across the Pacific. So --- like a banana, I may be yellow on the outside, but I'm white on the inside.

And it doesn't matter now --- not at all.

Kings Packing Company is shown here in the late 1940s. (CCHS)

When the United States military dropped the atomic bomb on Japan in 1945, Nampans, along with the rest of the nation, were relieved to think that the war was over. Besides rationing, shortages, prisoner of war camps and discrimination, World War II meant death. Fifty-seven Nampa men had been killed in the war.

World War II had been a holy war, and when the final bomb was dropped, almost no one questioned the morality of that action. "It was a time when everybody felt that America was right and invincible," recalled Dr. Harold Brown. "I don't remember any guilt over dropping the atomic bombs."

The men who came home from the war were anxious to return to normal. They displayed a quiet certainty. This was the generation that "came back and knew they were gonna make it," according to Dr. Brown. "There wasn't much zeal about it because there was no other side of the coin; that was just the way it was." Thus, Nampans displayed a great interest in continuing their educations, developing businesses, establishing families, buying homes, and acquiring material resources.

Recognizing that wartime production would be converted into peacetime industrial output, a group of Nampa businessmen made plans to actively solicit commercial enterprises for this area. Working with the Nampa Chamber of Commerce, these men began in 1947 to talk of expanding the industrial base of the town. Up to that time, Nampa's economy was almost totally dependent upon the agricultural community. That year the Nampa Chamber of Commerce purchased a small tract of land near Karcher junction,

These men rode in wheelbarrows as part of an Eagles parade in the 1940s. Frank Kibler rides in the front wheelbarrow. (Courtesy, Edith Williamson)

planning to utilize it as an industrial site.

In 1948, the Board of Directors of the Chamber of Commerce requested that the Industrial Committee undertake an exhaustive analysis of the potential for industrial development in the area. A year later, nineteen local businessmen formed the Nampa Industrial Corporation. The promoters sold stock for $100 a share and the corporation began operation with $8500. Incorporated on August 30, 1949, the Nampa Industrial Corporation planned to purchase land which could be resold to businesses at a reasonable price, thus encouraging the establishment of industries in the area and bringing new jobs and payrolls to the town.

By March of 1950, stock sales left the corporation with $15,200 on deposit. The Chamber of Commerce paid all expenses associated with operating the Nampa Industrial Corporation and stockholders were promised that money gained from the sale of stock would be used only for purchasing land. As its first purchase, the corporation bought the land owned by the Chamber which later became the site of Meridian Wood Products.

Windsor Lloyd was the first president of the Nampa Industrial Corporation. (Courtesy, Nampa City Hall)

Nampans crowded the streets to see a Farm-City Day parade in the late 1940s. (Courtesy, Ruth Allen)

In 1951, the corporation raised $33,700 to buy a sixty-two acre site to be set aside for industrial development. Fleetwood Trailer Corporation became the first major development on this land in 1957. When Fleetwood was not interested in purchasing ground, the corporation raised enough money through additional stock sales to construct a facility which was leased to Fleetwood.

During the next decade, the concept envisioned by the founders of the Nampa Industrial Corporation came to fruition. Numerous businesses including the Heston Metal Company, Albertson's Feed Mill and Hatchery, Hehr Manufacturing, Luekenga Construction Company, Mountain Bell, Broadmore Mobile Homes of Idaho, Northland Camps, Peterson Trucking Company, Ferdinand Metal Company, Sport King Campers, and Rain For Rent, either bought land or leased facilities on the first industrial site. By 1970, only two acres of land were left on the original site.

That year, the corporation purchased an additional twenty-nine acres of land, calling this the Second Addition. In 1971, the organization bought another twenty-nine acres comprising the Third Addition and in 1972, purchased an additional thirty-five acres,

Nampa in 1950

*Twelfth Avenue South
(Courtesy, Elaine
Chapin)*

*Second Street South
(Courtesy, Elaine
Chapin)*

*The Dewey Palace
Hotel (Courtesy Elaine
Chapin)*

First Street South
(Courtesy, Elaine Chapin)

The Lakeview Park Bowl
(Courtesy, Elaine Chapin)

Lakeview Park (Courtesy,
Elaine Chapin)

The Nampa Industrial Corporation was instrumental in encouraging industries to locate in Nampa in recent decades. Shown here is one of the N.I.C. sites. (Courtesy, Nampa Public Library)

Pacific Press, a Seventh-Day Adventist Publishing firm, moved to Nampa from California, opening its $6,750,000 facility in 1985. (Courtesy, Pacific Press)

designating this the Fourth Addition. During these years, many of the businesses which were leasing from the Nampa Industrial Corporation bought their facilities, making it possible for the corporation to purchase the additional land.

By April of 1974, the Nampa Industrial Corporation had invested approximately $1,236,400 in land, improvements and facilities. In the 1980s, businesses and industries continued to locate in or near the Nampa Industrial Corporation complex. Zilog, a computer company that manufactures integrated circuits, purchased ground from the corporation and completed construction

The Harris M200 web press at Pacific Press prints 32,000 sixteen- or thirty-two-page signatures per hour. Paper passes through the press at 1000 feet per minute. (Courtesy, Pacific Press)

of its facility in August of 1979. An addition was added to the building in 1984. Pacific Press, a Seventh-Day Adventist publishing firm, located in a forty-acre area adjacent to the NIC sites, constructing a 183,000-square-feet facility that cost $6,750,000 in 1984.

Catering to industrial concerns, Nampa encouraged the establishment of business enterprises in the area in the years following World War II. Consequently, the economy of the area became less dependent upon the agricultural community. In 1930, forty-five percent of those employed in Canyon County worked in agricultural jobs. By 1970, this figure decreased to a little over fourteen percent.

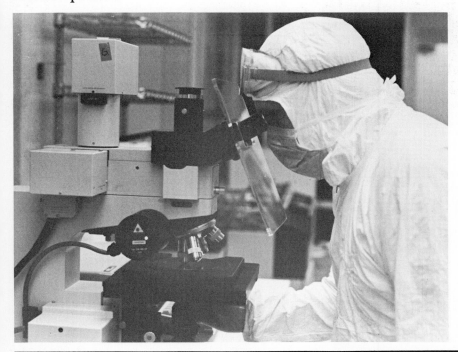

Zilog, a computer industry, located in Nampa in August of 1979. (Courtesy, Nampa Chamber of Commerce)

PFC HERBERT A. LITTLETON

Private First Class Herbert A. Littleton, USMCR, was presented the Congressional Medal of Honor posthumously by the President of the United States in the name of the Congress for service above and beyond the call of duty in Korea on April 22, 1951. While serving as a radio operator with an Artillery Forward Observation Team of Company C, First Battalion, Seventh Marines, First Marine Division (Reinforced), Littleton alerted the forward observation team when a well-concealed and numerically superior enemy force launched a night attack against his company. When an enemy hand grenade was thrown into his vantage point shortly after the arrival of the remainder of the team, he hurled himself on the deadly missile, absorbing its full impact. By this action, he lost his life, but saved the other members of his team from serious injury or death. (Courtesy, Nampa City Hall)

Nampa Casualties in World War II Include:

Glen S. Admyers
William F. Anson
Glenn L. Barnhart
Stanley E. Bohac
Loyal P. Bradley
Robert E. Brasfield
Donald S. Brown
Earl L. Brown
John E. Burt
Ernest T. Carlow
Roger G. Crain
Joe M. Divin
Lou J. Divin
Glen Dye
Arthur R. Elliot
Jesse J. Endicott
Lyle D. Feeny
Lyle A. Geisler
Fred Gillespie
Duane C. Glancy
Charles H. Goettling
John C. Gray
Kenneth A. Gray
William A. Haynes
Eldon Heston
Howard Heyman
John D. Holladay
James K. Horner
Donald L. Humpherys

Robert L. Jackson
Merlyn D. Johnson
Glenn R. Jones
Howard E. Lewis
Gilbert E. McCorkle
Richard C. Miles
Truman Miller
Richard Minden
Van N. Moad, Jr.
Dowayne W. Munster
Charles W. Murphy, Jr.
Norman O. Needham
Percy Neel
John M. Norquist
Leonard Parkinson
Robert D. Pinkerton
Howard Ramey, Jr.
Joe Francis Roofener
Charles F. Salek
Harry A. Sealy
Howard M. Spry
Harold Thompson
Lyle Tiffany
William M. Towery
Donald Lee Ward
Walter H. White
Elless G. Wright
Laddie John Zacek

Nampa Casualties in the Korean Conflict Include:

Ralph L. Harrison
Herbert A. Littleton
Donald Lee Munster
John White

IX
The Recent Decades:
1960 - 1985

The past two or three decades leading up to Nampa's centennial year have been active ones in terms of the growth and development of business enterprises, residential dwellings and city services in the town. However, the community has been influenced by the economic ups and downs of the nation on the whole.

Prior to the 1960s, Nampa maintained a central business district which provided most of the services required by the town's residents. In addition to retail establishments, professional offices, city government and city services were all generally located within the downtown business section. Neighborhood grocery stores constituted the major exception to this general rule. In the 1950s, one had only to go a few blocks in a residential area before coming upon a small, neighborhood grocery. Thirty to fifty of these "mom and pop" stores dominated the retail food business in Nampa before the advent of the supermarket in the 1960s.

The owner of one of these neighborhood stores, Wilbur Kirk of Holly Market, developed Nampa's first shopping center in the early 1960s. Walter Opp, contractor for the development, took out a building permit for $280,000 and construction began in October of 1962. Located between Roosevelt and Washington Avenues and Holly and Garland Streets in southeast Nampa, Holly Shopping Center opened in the spring of 1963 with a grocery store, drug store, laundry, barber shop, beauty shop, and professional offices. In the past twenty years, several additions have enlarged the original building.

At the same time that Holly Shopping Center was being developed, other business establishments were moving away from the downtown core. In May of 1965, the Safeway Grocery Store took out a building permit for $210,000 in order to build a store in the Owyhee Shopping Center which was being constructed on Twelfth Avenue Road near Lake Lowell Avenue. This complex of stores opened in December of 1965.

In August of the same year, Nampa's largest building project in the post-war period opened for business on Nampa-Caldwell

Facing Page: Jim Lemon was one of the first to undertake major renovation in the downtown area. In 1981 he completed construction of the First Street Market, restoring a structure which was built around 1910. (Courtesy, Jim Lemon)

Karcher Mall, Nampa's largest building project in the post-war period, opened in August of 1965. In 1985, after several expansions, sixty-five stores occupy 538,000 square feet in the enclosed shopping mall. (Courtesy, Nampa Chamber of Commerce)

First Street South between Twelfth and Thirteenth Avenues is the site of some of the recent downtown redevelopment. This historic area, earlier known as Main Street, bordered the block of the 1909 fire. (Courtesy, Jim Lemon)

Boulevard. Karcher Mall, planned and developed by the Daum Corporation, brought Nampa into the age of the one-stop, indoor shopping mall. From its inception, Karcher Mall has undergone several expansions, enlarging its floor space from 103,000 square feet to 538,000 square feet. In 1985, sixty-five stores occupied space in the mall, with several other retail concerns located nearby.

Such a development was bound to have an effect on Nampa's

downtown business district. Unable to compete with Karcher Mall and the outlying stores, the downtown area, once the dynamic center of the community, dwindled, until empty buildings and struggling retail stores dominated the region. Not until the 1980s did a combination of public and private funds give some promise of the revitalization of downtown Nampa.

After years of inactivity in the downtown area, in 1981, Jim Lemon followed a national trend toward redevelopment of historic structures by remodeling an old building on First Street South between Twelfth and Thirteenth Avenues. This $140,000 undertaking, called the First Street Market, provided space for a restaurant, retail stores and professional offices. This venture demonstrated that contemporary space could be carved out of historic structures in downtown Nampa.

In 1983, Lemon enlarged his project by renovating the C. Meister building which stands in the middle of the same block as First Street Market and in 1985, he began to renovate the W. Hardiman building which was originally constructed in 1909 and is between the two other structures. Overall, Lemon is spending a half million dollars on historic buildings in downtown Nampa.

The Little Kitchen occupies an area in the First Street Market, a major restoration project undertaken by Jim Lemon on Nampa's First Street South. (Courtesy, Jim Lemon)

In 1982, Dr. Harold Brown, Dr. Kenneth Droulard and Dr. Fred Plum formed a partnership called Longbranch Incorporated and bought the fire-gutted Longbranch Saloon, a vacant bowling alley next door and Gene's Lounge which occupied part of the bowling alley building. With these buildings as their core, the developers began the remodeling of Longbranch Station, a two-million dollar project which opened in 1984 with a business office, dress shop, gift shop and children's shoe store as the first tenants. They have been followed by a restaurant and more retail and office units. The three original buildings have been joined together as one structure with open spaces, skylights, balconies and oak trim.

Sidewalk and street improvements, new lighting and landscaping were also undertaken in the block which houses the Longbranch development. These projects were funded through the formation of a local improvement district (LID) which was requested by the block's property owners. The LID taxed the property owners approximately $150 per frontage foot in order to raise the money to revitalize the public areas.

Motivated by the enthusiasm of the Longbranch developers, other downtown business leaders joined together in the fall of 1982 to request formation of a downtown business improvement district (BID). Approved by the Nampa City Council, that taxing district assessed downtown merchants in a nine-square block area more than $20,000. This money was used to form a BID advisory board and publish a 45-page report, issued in September of 1983, which detailed plans for future downtown redevelopment. Bruce Flesher, a local businessman, chaired the fifteen-member committee which produced this report.

Proponents of downtown redevelopment outlined a three-year project costing 2.4 million dollars, but funding for the venture was uncertain until April of 1984 when the city of Nampa received a 1.04 million dollar community development block grant. These state-administered federal funds were to be used to reconstruct downtown streets, build parking areas, and make improvements in the nine-square-block downtown redevelopment area. Downtown property owners agreed to contribute $738,510, in addition to the grant, through assessments they voted upon themselves when they

Downtown street improvements are one phase of the renovation program which is underway in 1985 in the nine-square-block downtown redevelopment area. (Courtesy, Idaho Press-Tribune)

The 1974 Cinco De Mayo Festival at Lakeview Park was well attended by the Hispanic community of the town. In the 1980s, Hispanics comprise nine percent of the population in Nampa. While many Hispanics came to the Nampa area as farm laborers, today they contribute to all segments of the community, including cultural development, education, agriculture, government, health services and business. (ISHS, donated by the Idaho Statesman)

formed a series of local improvement districts. The rest of the project funding, twenty-six percent of the total, was planned from city and state resources. The city agreed to contribute $344,298, most of which was to be provided through labor and "in-kind" services from city crews. The state was to pay $295,601, mainly for improvements to state highways which serve as city arterials. The Eleventh Avenue railroad underpass was also to be widened by the state. The 2.4 million dollar project is scheduled for completion in 1986.

In addition to the Longbranch and the public improvements, several other private developers have made plans for major business development in the downtown area.

The late 1970s and early 1980s saw a surge of development in both residential and non-residential construction. During that period, approximately 2000 single family homes were built in the Nampa urban area. But when a nationwide economic slow-down

Fred Meyer, shown here under construction, is a six million dollar project, opening in Nampa during the last quarter of 1985. The 125,000 square foot shopping center will include a grocery store as well as numerous retail departments. (Courtesy, Idaho Press-Tribune)

followed this period, building permit statistics for the city of Nampa reflected the recessionary trend. However, by 1984, the picture improved and construction in the city rebounded. During that year, the building permits issued by the city totaled $19,510,745 in value, a record high for the previous fifteen years. The trend continued, for by July of 1985, almost thirteen million dollars of contruction had been undertaken in the town.

Community services, in particular health care services, also underwent major expansion in the 1960s. Prior to that decade, Nampa was served by doctors who generally functioned as family practioners. That began to change with the formation of a major group practice in Nampa. Interested in securing specialists for the Nampa-area, Dr. Joseph Saltzer joined together with Dr. Harold W. Brown, Dr. Robert E. Hay and Dr. E.R. Carlsson in June of 1961 to establish the Canyon Medical Center Physicians, later known as the Medical Center Physicians, P.A. In August of 1976, this clinic moved into a 1.2 million dollar structure adjacent to the newly constructed Mercy Medical Center. In 1984, the developers added 20,000 square feet to the clinic's building. With twenty-eight physicians in the group, the Medical Center Physicians have become the largest medical clinic in the state of Idaho.

Mercy Medical Center, founded in 1917 by the Sisters of Mercy, was initially located in a brick building on Sixteenth Avenue and Ninth Street South, near St. Paul's Catholic Church, grade school and convent. On September 17, 1968, the hospital opened a new 114-bed facility at 1512 Twelfth Avenue Road and changed its name from Mercy Hospital to Mercy Medical Center. It became a community hospital with a board composed largely of lay members, although it retained its Roman Catholic affiliation.

As Mercy Medical Center expanded its facilities, developers constructed a large complex of physicians' office buildings directly across Twelfth Avenue Road from the hospital. Again, professional services joined business enterprises in moving away from the center core of the town.

Mercy Hospital, founded in 1917 by the Sisters of Mercy, opened a new 114-bed facility at 1512 Twelfth Avenue Road and changed its name to Mercy Medical Center in September of 1968. (Photo by Jim Thomas)

Dr. and Mrs. T. E. Mangum, Sr. founded Samaritan Hospital, adjacent to the Northwest Nazarene College campus, in 1920. They were interested not only in providing medical care for the town of Nampa but in training nurses to serve as medical missionaries. The first class of nursing students graduated in 1930.

After serving the community for forty-seven years, the hospital closed its doors in 1967, although many of its dedicated supporters continued an attempt to raise funds for a new or remodeled structure. When this no longer appeared feasible, the bulk of the money raised was turned over to Nampa Christian High School. The hospital building was sold to Northwest Nazarene College and, after extensive remodeling, became the school's Department of Fine Arts.

City government has also witnessed much activity during the past few decades. Ernie Starr served as mayor of Nampa from May of 1961 to December of 1981, overseeing many changes in the town and in city services during this time. Several highlights stand out during his tenure in office.

Three major construction projects relating to Nampa streets took place in the 1960s and 1970s. In 1961 when the State Highway Department and the Federal Highway Administration were building the interstate freeway past Nampa, the city was responsible for providing adequate highway connectors to the freeway. Thanks to the efforts of Senator Frank Church and Congresswoman Gracie Pfost, the city received Federal Aid Secondary (FAS) funds in the amount of $100,000, to build the highway connecting the town to the Franklin interchange. Also in 1961, the city started developing a plan to rebuild the Sixteenth Avenue underpass. By 1969 the project began, again utilizing federal highway construction funds. The new overpass, which cost over a million dollars to build, was officially opened in May of 1970. In the 1970s, federal FAS funds were used again to widen and rebuild a couple of sections of Twelfth Avenue in the downtown area. Citing this start, the city convinced the State Highway Department to rebuild and widen the rest of Twelfth Avenue South and the street improvements in that area became a cooperative project between the city and the state.

City services, in particular the sewage treatment system of the city, have influenced the capability of Nampa to support industrial enterprises in the area. In 1964, the citizens of Nampa approved a bond issue to expand the city's sewer plant. After the plant was rebuilt, the city made the mistake of trying to treat too much industrial waste, overloading the capability of the plant and generating an obnoxious odor in the community. Thus, in 1978, when the sewer treatment plant needed updating again, the voters approved a second bond issue which furnished ten percent of the eighteen-million-dollar project. Seventy-five percent of the funding was provided through a federal grant with the state picking up the additional fifteen percent of the funding. By the time this sewer treatment plant was completed in 1982, Nampa had the largest and most modern treatment plant in Idaho. Designed to process 11.8 milllion gallons of sewage per day, currently the average daily flow amounts to less than half of that capacity.

Nampa was one of the first communities in the State of Idaho to promote orderly community development through planning and zoning. In 1938, the city council approved Nampa's original zoning ordinance. This ordinance was repealed and the current

Ernie Starr served as mayor of Nampa from May of 1961 to December of 1981, overseeing many changes in the town and in city services during this time period. (Courtesy, Nampa City Hall)

Annie Laurie Bird, a well-known history teacher and Nampa historian, spent years researching and publishing information about Nampa's past, culminating her work with a book about Nampa, My Hometown, published in 1968. (Courtesy, ISHS)

The Idaho Free Press, started in April of 1919, became the Idaho Press-Tribune when the newspaper merged with the Caldwell Tribune in July of 1980. In the fall of the same year, the newspaper moved to its new facility on Midland Boulevard. (Courtesy, Idaho Press-Tribune)

Comprehensive Zoning Ordinance adopted in 1971. In 1969, the city endorsed its first comprehensive community plan which was amended and updated in 1977. These ordinances have established logical patterns of land use based on the needs and desires of Nampa's citizens.

In the early 1970s, when Congress instigated the Federal Revenue Sharing Program, Nampa decided to utilize the funding for major capital improvements and not for any regular budget needs. Major projects funded by revenue-sharing over the past several years include installation of a city-wide sprinkler irrigation system, construction of a new police station and building of a new city hall.

The old city hall, a two-story cream-colored brick building located on the corner of Twelfth Avenue and Second Street South,

KIVI, Channel 6 television, an ABC affiliate, began broadcasting from Nampa in February of 1974 from a mobile unit. In 1975 the station moved into this building. (Courtesy, KIVI-TV)

opened in the fall of 1910. In the 1960s and 1970s, the city council frequently discussed the need for a new facility, but the voters of Nampa twice rejected bond issues requiring a two-thirds vote which would have funded construction of a new building.

In 1980, when a suit was filed against the city by a handicapped citizen who complained that the stairs at the old city hall denied him access to meetings, a district court order forced the council to evacuate the council chambers in the old building. After months of cramped sessions in the courtroom of the county building on Ninth Avenue and Second Street South, where many people had to stand in the hallway, the council voted to use revenue sharing funds to construct a new city hall.

The city had already obtained a site for the building. After the Nampa School District built two new junior high schools, the old Nampa High School which had served as West Junior High in its later years, sat vacant. When the school district found it difficult to sell the property, officials offered it to the city at a reduced price of $350,000, which was $100,000 less than its appraised value, providing it would be utilized for the benefit of the community. The city and the school district completed negotiations on the parcel in February of 1977. The old school building which was showing the effects of age, was torn down, but the gymnasium was retained for community use and a ball field was developed on part of the property.

Construction of the new 1.2 million dollar city hall was completed on this site in August of 1982. The new municipal headquarters includes sixteen thousand square feet on its main floor with an unfinished basement containing 7300 square feet. The new City Council chambers feature a theater-style auditorium with a seating capacity of a little over a hundred. The building was designed so that a second floor could be added in the future. The city sold the old city hall property on Twelfth Avenue to a developer who planned to restore the structure, leaving the outer design of the building intact.

Winston K. Goering was elected mayor of Nampa in November of 1981. (Courtesy, Nampa City Hall)

The city council chamber in the new city hall features a theater-style auditorium with a seating capacity of a little over a hundred. (Photo by Jim Thomas)

In 1985, the Nampa Public Library restored the historic E. H. Dewey store, providing an addition to the building which doubles the library's square footage. (Photo by Jim Thomas)

As Nampa enters its centennial year, several civic projects are underway. A veteran's memorial, commemorating Nampa citizens who gave their lives for their country, has been constructed by volunteer labor on the City Hall grounds. Nampa Public Library has carefully restored the historic E. H. Dewey store, providing an addition which doubles the library's square footage. This historic restoration project confirms the reputation of the library as being one of a limited number of enterprises in town interested in preserving old buildings. The addition adjoins the old First Security bank building, built in 1919, which was remodeled in 1966 for library use after the city outgrew the old Carnegie Library building. And, finally, the city has encouraged private contributors to support the development of a one and a quarter million dollar 18-hole golf course on land near the Idaho State School and Hospital. The volunteer effort was undertaken after the voters of Nampa in 1982 overwhelmingly defeated a bond issue which would have funded the golf course construction. Over 1200 people have donated labor, material or money to the project which is scheduled for completion in 1986.

When Alexander Duffes founded Nampa, it was a small settlement in the midst of sagebrush connected to the rest of the world by the railroad. Now, Nampa, like other towns its size across the nation, is more than a community unto itself; it is part of a larger whole, connected to the country and the world not only through transportation networks, but also through television, satellites, and the wonders of modern technology. While Nampa has grown larger, the world has seemingly grown smaller, and this in turn has affected the character of the town. No longer isolated, Nampa reads the same news that is read in the midwest or on the east coast of the United States. Its citizens easily travel from the Nampa area to various parts of the world. The economic ups and downs of the nation influence the local business scene.

Nonetheless, Nampa retains characteristics that belong uniquely to the town. One of these is its history. No other town has Nampa's past.

The summer reading program at the Nampa Public Library is a popular attraction. It culminates each year with a special party in the park, which in 1985, featured hats of many shapes and sizes. (Courtesy, Idaho Press-Tribune)

Left: Wendell Christensen has coordinated the volunteer effort for constructing a 1.25 million dollar 18-hole golf course on land near the Idaho State School and Hospital. (Courtesy, Idaho Press-Tribune)

Nampa Casualities in the War in Vietnam Include:

Gerald Lee Baldwin
Jess Burton Boicourt, Jr.
Albara Quezada Garcias
Kay Kazu Kimura
Lynn Randall
Jimmy Lee Ward
Edward Joseph Weidenbach

Lake Lowell reflects the scenic beauty of nature in the Nampa area. (Photo by Jim Thomas)

BIBLIOGRAPHY

GENERAL REFERENCES:

Bird, Annie Laurie. *Boise, the Peace Valley.* Caldwell: Caxton Printers, Ltd., 1934.

_____. *My Home Town.* Caldwell: Caxton Printers, Ltd., 1968.

Cottingham, F. G. "History of Nampa and Vicinity." Unpublished manuscript, Nampa, 1911-1912. Nampa Public Library Northwest Collection.

CHAPTER REFERENCES:
CHAPTER 1

NAMPA'S BIRTH
Caldwell Tribune, October 30, 1885, February 20, 1886, March 27, 1886, April 3, 1886, May 1, 1886, July 10, 1886, October 2, 1886.

Herndon, Ellen Boulton. *I Remember Idaho: My Childhood on Boulton Farm.* Claremont, California: By Esther Boulton Black, 1972.

The Idaho Statesman (Boise, Idaho), January 10, 1901.

Kiser, William J. *Idaho Homestead.* Huntsville, Alabama: The Strode Publishers, 1982.

Mock, Fred. "Kiwanis Club Luncheon Speech," July 1936. "Fire of 1909" file, Annie Laurie Bird Collection, Northwest Nazarene College.

Nampa Leader-Herald, October 17, 1905, November 9, 1906, December 14, 1906, February 15, 1907, March 19, 1907, January 21, 1908, January 28, 1908, May 7, 1909, May 14, 1909, January 18, 1910, August 5, 1910.

Sappington, Roger E. *The Brethren Along the Snake River: A History of the Church of the Brethren in Idaho and Western Montana.* Elgin, Illinois: The Brethren Press, 1966.

CHAPTER II

COLONEL W. H. DEWEY AND THE DEWEY PALACE
"Dewey and Dewey Palace" file Annie Laurie Bird Collection, Northwest Nazarene College.

Fastabend, Faith. "William Dewey's Darkest Days." Unpublished thesis, Boise State University, no date.

BUSINESS DEVELOPMENT, 1900 - 1910
Nampa Leader-Herald, October 1905 - June 1909.

FIRST SUGAR BEET FACTORY
Nampa Leader-Herald, January 16, 1906, October 29, 1909, February 8, 1910, August 12, 1910, September 30, 1913.

THE CRESCENT BREWERY
Lockman, Adah. Interview by Lucille M. McShane. Nampa, Idaho. June 20, 1973.

Nampa Leader-Herald, January 26, 1906, June 21, 1910, June 24, 1910, July 26, 1910, August 5, 1910.

THE FIRE OF 1909
Hart, Arthur A. "Fire 'Leveled' Nampa in '09," *Idaho Statesman,* June 28, 1971.

Mock, Fred. "Kiwanis Club Luncheon Speech," July 1936.

"Fire of 1909" file, Annie Laurie Bird Collection, Northwest Nazarene College.

Murray, Harold E. Interview by Evelyn Hagelin. Nampa, Idaho. May 11, 1974.

Nampa Leader-Herald, April 13, 1909, May 18, 1909, June 8, 1909, June 29, 1909, July 5, 1909, July 9, 1909.

CHAPTER III

PROHIBITION
Nampa Leader-Herald, January 18, 1910, January 28, 1910, February 11, 1910, April 1, 1910, April 12, 1910, May 3, 1910, May 6, 1910, May 13, 1910, January 3, 1911, January 27, 1911, January 31, 1911, February 28, 1911, April 4, 1911, July 21, 1911, July 28, 1911, August 22, 1911, September 1, 1911, September 5, 1911, September 8, 1911, January 9, 1912, September 23, 1913.

BANK OF NAMPA
Nampa Leader-Herald, September 2, 1913, September 30, 1913, October 7, 1913, February 3, 1914, February 17, 1914, May 15, 1914, July 31, 1914, October 13, 1914, December 11, 1914.

CITY POLITICS
Nampa Leader-Herald, July 8, 1910, July 19, 1910, July 22, 1910, July 29, 1910, February 3, 1911, February 14, 1911, February 24, 1911, February 28, 1911, March 3, 1911, March 17, 1911, March 24, 1911, March 28, 1911, March 31, 1911, April 4, 1911, April 7, 1911, September 26, 1911, October 9, 1911, December 12, 1911, March 21, 1913, April 4, 1913, January 20, 1914, February 3, 1914, March 26, 1915, April 16, 1915, April 20, 1915, April 23, 1915, April 27, 1915, April 30, 1915.

THE INTERURBAN
Anketell, Ben. Interview by Marie

Wade. Nampa, Idaho. May 31, 1985.

Bird, Annie Laurie. "Valley Once Had Trolley Line," *Idaho Free Press,* July 6, 1963.

Hostetler, Mrs. Dessie. Interview by Helen M. Payne. Nampa, Idaho. June 16, 1973.

Nampa Leader-Herald, August 12, 1910, September 2, 1913, September 5, 1913.

Waigand, Ben. Interview by Camille Beaubien. Nampa, Idaho. May 28, 1985.

AUTOMOBILES

Brandt, John. Interview by Herbert Douglass. Nampa, Idaho. May 16, 1985.

Jacobsen, George Jr. Interview by Marie Wade. Nampa, Idaho. June 12, 1985.

Mangum, Dr. Bob. Interview by Frances Coyle. Nampa, Idaho. May 30, 1985.

Nampa Leader-Herald, June 10, 1910, August 2, 1910, August 12, 1910, October 29, 1909, March 14, 1911, March 17, 1911, March 21, 1911, July 18, 1911, September 2, 1913, June 3, 1914, June 16, 1914, July 31, 1914, August 18, 1914, September 1, 1914, March 20, 1917.

Waigand, Ben. Interview by Camille Beaubien. Nampa, Idaho. May 28, 1985.

CHAPTER IV

NORTHWEST NAZARENE COLLEGE

Culver, Thelma B. "Eugene Emerson, Founder, Northwest Nazarene College." Founders' Day Address, Northwest Nazarene College, Nampa, Idaho, September 28, 1973.

DeLong, Russell V. and Albert Harper. *Northwest Nazarene College: Silver Anniversary, Twenty-five Years of Progress, 1913 - 1938.* Nampa, Idaho: Northwest Nazarene College, 1938.

"Northwest Nazarene College: The

Founding Years," unpublished manuscript, no date.

Riley, Dr. John E. Interview by Mrs. Ralph Little. Nampa, Idaho. July 23, 1973.

Riley, Mrs. John. Interview by Mrs. Ralph Little. Nampa, Idaho. August 22, 1973.

IDAHO STATE SCHOOL AND HOSPITAL

"A Brief History of the Idaho State School and Hospital," unpublished manuscript by the Idaho State School and Hospital, no date.

Gwilliam, Irene G. "A History of the Beginnings of Idaho State School and Hospital," unpublished manuscript from the Canyon County Historical Society, no date.

Idaho Press-Tribune (Nampa, Idaho), May 15, 1985.

Idaho Statesman (Boise, Idaho), March 7, 1982.

Nampa Leader-Herald, February 14, 1911, May 5, 1911, May 9, 1911, March 26, 1915.

CHAPTER V

WORLD WAR I AND THE 1920s

Brandt, John. Interview by Herbert Douglass. Nampa, Idaho. May 16, 1985.

Hartman, Howard. Interview by Jaci Wilkins. Boise, Idaho. May 17, 1985.

Idaho Free Press (Nampa, Idaho), September 19, 1920, September 21, 1920.

Murray, Harold E. Interview by Evelyn Hagelin. Nampa, Idaho. May 11, 1974.

Nampa Leader-Herald, February 20, 1917, April 21, 1914, August 7, 1914, September 11, 1914, February 9, 1917, March 27, 1917, March 30, 1917, April 3, 1917, April 6, 1917, May 18, 1917, May 29, 1917, June 1, 1917, June 8, 1917, June 15, 1917, June 22, 1917, August 6, 1920, August 10, 1920, September 10, 1920, September

14, 1920, September 21, 1920, September 24, 1920, May 10, 1921, June 21, 1921, June 24, 1921, June 15, 1923, June 22, 1923, June 26, 1923.

Waigand, Ben. Interview by Camille Beaubien. Nampa, Idaho. May 28, 1985.

CHAPTER VI

EARLY AGRICULTURE

Caldwell, H. H. and Merle Wells. "Economic and Ecological History Support Study: A Case Study of Federal Expenditures on a Water and Related Land Resources Project: Boise Project, Idaho and Oregon." Boise, Idaho: Idaho Water Resorce Board, June 1974.

Department of the Interior. "U.S. Reclamation Service History of the Boise Project, Idaho from the beginning to 1912." "Irrigation" pamphlet file, Idaho State Historical Society Archives, Boise, Idaho.

Henshall, Mary. "Haying in the '20s," unpublished manuscript, 1985.

Lovin, Hugh T. "The Farmer Revolt in Idaho, 1914-1922." 20 *Idaho Yesterdays* (Fall, 1976): 2-15

Murphy, Paul L. "Early Irrigation in the Boise Valley." *Pacific Northwest Quarterly* 44 (October 1953) : 177-84.

THE NONPARTISAN LEAGUE

Lovin, Hugh T. "A. C. Townley's 'North Dakota Plan' on Trial in Idaho, 1917 - 1922." Paper presented at the Pacific Northwest History Association Conference, Boise, Idaho, April 1976.

Nampa Leader-Herald, May 8, 1917, July 13, 1917, August 28, 1917, October 19, 1920, November 2, 1920, September 9, 1921, November 10, 1922, November 7, 1924, November 5, 1926, November 9, 1928.

THE IDAHO FREE PRESS

Idaho Free Press (Nampa, Idaho), April 9, 1919 - March 7, 1920.

Idaho Statesman (Boise, Idaho), April 12, 1919, May 3, 1919.

Nampa Leader-Herald, April 15, 1919, May 6, 1919, May 20, 1919.

CHAPTER VII

THE DEPRESSION

Anketell, Ben. Interview by Marie Wade. Nampa, Idaho. May 31, 1985.

Blakeslee, Kern. Interview by Kathy Hamlett. Nampa, Idaho. April 19, 1985.

Bowles, Leonard. Interview by Ray Larson. Nampa, Idaho. May 22, 1985.

Brandt, John. Interview by Herbert Douglass. Nampa, Idaho. May 16, 1985.

Burri, Elmer. Interview by Lois M. Smith. Nampa, Idaho. May 22, 1985.

Castagneto, Lloyd. Interview by Craig Castagneto. Nampa, Idaho. May 29, 1985.

Castagneto, William. Interview by Jaci Wilkins. Nampa, Idaho. May 20, 1985.

Coyle, Willis and Frances. Interview by Minnie Keim. Nampa, Idaho. June 2, 1985.

Crill, Elmo. Interview by Sue Stark. Nampa, Idaho. June 6, 1985.

"Depression" file, Annie Laurie Bird Collection, Northwest Nazarene College.

Ferdinand, Bob. Interview by Kris Rodine. Nampa, Idaho. May 23, 1985.

Goering, Margaret Keim. Interview by Frances Coyle. Nampa, Idaho. May 29, 1985.

Hartman, Howard. Interview by Jaci Wilkins. Boise, Idaho. May 17, 1985.

Idaho Free Press (Nampa, Idaho), March 6, 1933, March 8, 1933, March 9, 1933, March 10, 1933, March 15, 1933, October 11, 1935, October 15, 1935, October 18, 1935, October 22, 1935, August 24, 1937.

Isgrigg, Effie. Interview by Beverly

Clark. Nampa, Idaho. August 16, 1985.

Jacobsen, George. Interview by Marie Wade. Nampa, Idaho. June 12, 1985.

Johnson, Sumner. Interview by Ken Harward. Nampa, Idaho. May 16, 1985.

Mangum, Dr. Bob. Interview by Frances Coyle. Nampa, Idaho. May 30, 1985.

Murray, Harold E. Interview by Evelyn Hagelin. Nampa, Idaho. May 11, 1974.

Robb, Harry. Interview by Kevin Nelson. Nampa, Idaho. May 16, 1985.

Stark, Flossie. Interview by Camille Beaubien. Nampa, Idaho. May 23, 1985.

Waigand, Ben. Interview by Camille Beaubien. Nampa, Idaho. May 28, 1985.

Ware, Ed. Interview by Dr. Joseph Mayfield. Nampa, Idaho. May 21, 1985.

CHAPTER VIII

WORLD WAR II AND ITS AFTERMATH

Brandt, John. Interview by Herbert Douglass. Nampa, Idaho. May 16, 1985.

Brown, Dr. Harold. Interview by Kris Rodine. Nampa, Idaho. May 23, 1985.

Brown, Marguerite. Interview by Terry White. Nampa, Idaho. June 17, 1985.

Castagneto, William. Interview by Jaci Wilkins. Nampa, Idaho. May 20, 1985.

Crill, Elmo. Interview by Sue Stark. Nampa, Idaho. June 6, 1985.

Henshall, Mary Fujii, unpublished manuscript, June, 1985.

Idaho Press-Tribune (Nampa, Idaho), November 11, 1984.

Jacobsen, George. Interview by Marie Wade. Nampa, Idaho. June 12, 1985.

"Nampa Industrial Complex." Pamphlet printed by the Nampa Chamber of Commerce, April,

1974.

Robb, Harry. Interview by Kevin Nelson. Nampa, Idaho. May 16, 1985.

Shaw, Bill and Frieda. Interview by Beverly Clark. Nampa, Idaho. May 17, 1985.

Stark, Flossie. Interview by Camille Beaubien. Nampa, Idaho. May 23, 1985.

Ware, Ed. Interview by Dr. Joseph Mayfield. Nampa, Idaho. May 21, 1985.

CHAPTER IX

RECENT DECADES

Idaho Press-Tribune (Nampa, Idaho), September 10, 1982, February 3, 1984, July 6, 1984, August 19, 1984, November 2, 1984, February 7, 1985, April 4, 1985, June 13, 1985.

Star, Ernest E., unpublished manuscript, August, 1985.

ACKNOWLEDGMENTS

Many people have made this book possible. It took vision and courage for Ken Harward and the Nampa Centennial Committee to undertake such a major project. They also provided unhesitating support during the time that it took to put the book together.

The Nampa Public Library freely shared of its collection of historic Nampa pictures. Gerda Ruppert, director of the library, coordinated the work of collecting and organizing the pictures for the illustrations in the book. Thanks also goes to Karen Ganske who spent many hours working with the pictures and to the other members of the Nampa Public Library staff who assisted in this effort.

Kathy Hamlett, curator of the Canyon County Historical Society, also played a major role in gathering pictures for the book. She helped collect pictures from Nampans and generously shared of the resources of the Canyon County Historical Society. Many of the original prints used in the book came from the Canyon County Historical Society (CCHS) collection. The Idaho State Historical Society (ISHS) also loaned photographs to be used in the book. Thanks goes to their staff for providing valuable assistance. Thanks also to the many individuals who took apart their scrapbooks to provide us with pictures representative of Nampa's past. These people have played an important role in helping to portray the history of the town.

Kevin Nelson spent untold hours putting the book together. He was responsible for the design and layout work. Jim Thomas from Viewpoint did most of the photography work. He aptly copied old photographs, doing whatever was necessary to make them useable for the book. Also he took several of the contemporary pictures, donating his time and talents to this centennial project. Kevin and Jim were great to work with.

Gayle Moore did the editing and proofreading, undertaking these tasks in her usual thorough and cheerful manner. Marguerite Brown provided research material for the "Recent Decades" chapter and also served as a reader for the text of the book as it was being written.

Many people participated in the oral history project which started as an outgrowth of the research effort for this book and became a major undertaking with tremendous value of its own. Fifty-six Nampans willingly shared their experiences and allowed their recollections to be recorded for the posterity of Nampa. The interviewers were Camille Beaubien, Marguerite Brown, Craig and Linda Castagneto, Dick Claiborne, Beverly Clark, Russ Cooke, Frances Coyle, Dr. Herb Douglass, Kathy Hamlett, Ken Harward, Janet Hay, Julie Jolley, Minnie Keim, Ray Larson, Dr. Joseph Mayfield, Kevin Nelson, Kris Rhodine, Ethyl Schultz, Lois Smith, Sue Stark, Florence Taylor, Eva Verner, Marie Wade, Terry White, and Jaci Wilkins. Camille Beaubien, Becky Cooper, Gayle Cooper, Lisa Moore, and Jan Parker-Ross spent numerous hours in the tedious task of transcribing the interviews.

Mary Terese McConnell and the Idaho State School provided information on the history of the institution. Edith Lancaster, Myron Finkbeiner and Helen Wilson contributed information and pictures for the history of Northwest Nazarene College.

The people at Nampa City Hall, including Camille Beaubien, Daryl LeDuc, Dee Mereness and Norm Holm, were marvelous to work with. Their encouragement and assistance are greatly appreciated. Dr. Herb Douglass, Dave Lawson and the people of Pacific Press were patient and supportive as they worked with us and undertook the task of printing the book.

The *Idaho Statesman* gave permission to reprint pictures originally taken by the *Statesman*. The *Idaho Press-Tribune* gave permission to quote from the newspaper. The assistance of these people has helped make the writing of a history of Nampa easier.

To everyone who has provided support and encouragement, this is your book. Thank you.

Lynda Campbell Clark
October, 1985